SERVICE QUALITY
IN ACADEMIC LIBRARIES

Information Management, Policy, and Services
Peter Hernon, Editor

For Information Specialists
Howard White, Marcia Bates, and Patrick Wilson
Public Library Youth Services: A Public Policy Approach ʼ
Holly G. Willett

In Preparation:
Meaning and Method in Information Studies
Ian Cornelius
Reclaiming the American Library Past: Writing the Women In
Suzanne Hildenbrand (Editor)
Knowledge Diffusion in the U.S. Aerospace Industry
Thomas E. Pinelli, et al.

SERVICE QUALITY IN ACADEMIC LIBRARIES

Peter Hernon
*Simmons College,
 Boston;
Victoria University of
 Wellington, New Zealand*

Ellen Altman
*Formerly of the University of
 Arizona, Tucson*

Ablex Publishing Corporation
Norwood, New Jersey

Printed in the United States of America.

Library of Congress Cataloging-in-Publication Data

Hernon, Peter.
    Service quality in academic libraries / Peter Hernon, Ellen
Altman.
        p.   cm. — (Information management, policy, and services)
    Includes bibliographical references (p.) and index.
    ISBN 1-56750-209-1 (cloth). — ISBN 1-56750-210-5 (paper : alk.
paper)
    1. Academic libraries—United States. 2. Libraries and students—
United States. 3. Libraries and scholars—United States.
I. Altman, Ellen. II. Title. III. Series.
Z675.U5H55 1995
025.5'2777—dc20   95-42989
                                                   CIP

Ablex Publishing Corporation
355 Chestnut Street
Norwood, NJ 07648

Contents

LIST OF FIGURES

LIST OF TABLES

Acknowledgments

We wish to thank all the librarians and students who participated in the research. They provided invaluable insights and were most generous with their time. We also appreciate the help Dora Suarez provided with Appendices A and B, the careful reading of the manuscript by Helene Woodhams, and the patience of Allan Pratt and Elinor Hernon, who endured lengthy discussions of service quality. Allan Pratt also kindly prepared figures for Chapters 2, 6, and 7. We also thank Anne Trowbridge of Ablex Publishing Corp. for invaluable assistance in preparation of the manuscript for publication.

We are indebted to various publishers for granting permission to use material from their works:

Bergquist, William. "Redefining Quality in the Context of Access." *Quality through Access, Access with Quality: The New Imperative for Higher Education,* p. 70. Copyright 1995 by Jossey-Bass Inc., Publishers.

Bergquist, William. "Critical Role for Campus Leaders." *Quality through Access, Access with Quality: The New Imperative for Higher Education,* p. 273. Copyright 1995 by Jossey-Bass Inc., Publishers.

Goulding, Mary. "Minimum Standards as a First Step Toward Evaluation of Reference Services in a Multitype System," in *Evaluation of Public Services and Public Services Personnel* edited by Bryce Allen, 103–123. Allerton Park Institute, Number 32. Urbana-Champaign, IL: Graduate School of Library and Information Science, University of Illinois, [1991]. (Quote from page 109).

Mackay, Harvey. "Hospitals Could Learn Plenty from Market Oriented Firms." *The Arizona Republic* (April 8, 1995), p. E6. United Feature Syndicate as the copyright holder. Reprinted with permission.

McDonald, Joseph A. and Lynda Basney Micikas, *Academic Libraries: The Dimensions of Their Effectiveness,* reprinted with permission of Greenwood Publishing Group, Inc., Westport, CT. Copyright © 1994. Joseph A. McDonald, *Academic Libraries.* Greenwood Press, 88 Post Road West, Westport, CT, 1994. An imprint of Greenwood Publishing Group, Inc.

Measuring Institutional Performance in Higher Education, edited by William F. Massy & Joel Meyerson, Peterson's Princeton, NJ.

Preface

Poor quality, fewer customers, budget cuts, fewer jobs, and serious competition from mega bookstores, document delivery services, and online information networks—such prospects represent the worst nightmare for librarians, but all these prospects currently confront academic and other libraries. One might ask, for instance, how many students really do use the library and for what reasons? Clearly, the quality of service delivered by libraries is a topic of increasing interest and concern among all members of the library community, as we would like everyone to believe that libraries are operated "by people who actually like their work and want to help you, which is to say that they're exactly the opposite of the people who work for the Registry of Motor Vehicles" (Craig, 1995, p. 78).

Service quality is an issue separate from internal observations of effectiveness and efficiency, and cannot adequately be conveyed by output and performance measures. Considerations of service quality require librarians to regard management and the provision of service from an entirely new perspective—that is, from the viewpoint of the library user for whom the outcome of a trip to the library has far greater relevance than the institution's outputs.

This book examines service quality, identifies its essential elements (including electronic service delivery), and discusses ways in which service quality can be assessed quantitatively and qualitatively. *Service Quality in Academic Libraries,* based on a two-year research study, encourages every manager to consider the impact of accountability on the library's role within the larger organization. It identifies simple and practical methods by which to implement measures representing service quality and narrow the gap between library services and customer expectations.

Peter Hernon & Ellen Altman
July, 1995

Chapter 1

The Customer Is the Key

People want what they want when they want it.
They don't want something else,
they don't want less than they want,
and they certainly don't want it at some other time.

—Forsha, 1992, p. 3

Librarians have, for years, lamented their inabilities to depict library services as vital to the academic community and especially to those responsible for funding the library. As we listened to academic librarians in preparation of Chapter 4 we were struck by their frustration at failing to find the magic key that would prove the worth of their efforts in a definitive way to college and university administrators, thus unlocking the treasure chest of funding.

There is no magic key. Moreover, measures to indicate the impact of the library on the campus community are quite obvious, although perhaps not widely recognized. Almost every academic library claims its mission is to support the curriculum and the research activities of the university's faculty. Therefore, the degree of the library's success in supporting teaching and research would be a good indicator of its contribution to the institution. The following simple measures, if reported annually, would be a reasonably accurate reflection of the library's contributions toward teaching and research:

- The percentage of courses using the reserve reading room;
- The percentage of students enrolled in those courses who actually checked out reserve materials;

1

- The percentage of courses requiring term papers based on materials from the library;
- The number of students involved in those courses;
- The percentage of students who checked out library materials;
- The percentage of faculty who checked out library materials;
- The percentage of courses using reading packets based on materials photocopied from the library's collection;
- The number of articles and books published by faculty members; and
- The number of references cited in faculty publications from materials contained in the collection.

However, we are unaware of any academic library that has ever published any such data to show how it supports teaching and research. Nor do we know of any professional organizations specifically concerned with academic libraries that have ever offered any suggestions on how to describe, in a comprehensive manner, the importance of the library's support of the college or university's mission. The few studies done in the 1930s and 1940s that examined the relationship between students' use of the library and their grade point averages failed to find any significant statistical relationships. Therefore, any measures that directly relate to the curriculum and research were discarded long ago.

It is not surprising that most academic libraries do not use measures directly related to their mission, because colleges and universities, in general, do not attempt to measure how well they educate students and create or advance knowledge—their ostensible mission. Instead, colleges and universities, and their attendant departments, focus on their perceived reputations vis-à-vis the reputations of those institutions that they consider peers. In this way, both the institutions and their libraries avoid meaningful measures of performance.

TRADITIONAL MEASURES OF LIBRARY PERFORMANCE

Most libraries collect information on circulation statistics and transaction totals (the number of interactions between employees and library materials and between employees and library users) processed in each department. Most departmental reports, however, fail to include anything about quality. Reports from cataloging, reference, and circulation departments typically include nothing beyond the number of transactions between staff, materials, and customers or how resources (dollars and staff time) were used to buy and process materials and services. These reports ostensibly are intended to *imply* effectiveness or quality. In reality there is no connection, because these numbers do not reflect the human dimension involved in the interactions.

Transaction counts reveal nothing about the ways in which a library unit pleased or disappointed customers. In fact, it is doubtful that units having no direct public contact ever consider library users at all. Indeed, one technical services person who participated in a focus group (for Chapter 4) insisted that standards of cataloging as determined by the Library of Congress constituted the criteria to satisfy; these standards are more important than the people using the library. This kind of thinking, focused on cataloging for the sake of cataloging, emphasizes technical perfection rather than provision of materials to customers; large cataloging backlogs certainly reflect a vast indifference to the library's customers.

A library's quality has traditionally been measured by the annual statistics that it reports to the university administration, to organizations such as the Association of Research Libraries (ARL), and to various other accreditation groups. These statistics include the size of the annual budget and the number of items on which the funds were spent, categorized by type, such as the number of volumes added or librarians employed. Library administrators often compare these transactions and input statistics with those of other libraries that they consider peers. For example, the ARL's members carefully peruse its annual statistics to see if their rankings have changed since the previous year. The libraries' concern with these rankings is quite understandable because they are the barometer of reputations in higher education's pecking order. However, they say nothing meaningful about the quality of service rendered, because they focus almost exclusively on the library's internal operations rather than on its customers. However, libraries exist only to serve customers, not to be museums of graphic records or places of employment. Only customers justify the existence of a library.

Higher education administrators are looking for their own magic key, a way by which to demonstrate the value and contributions of their institutions. They must answer increasingly pointed questions about the benefits of the hundreds of millions of dollars spent on higher education from legislators pressed to appropriate more money for health care, elementary and secondary schools, and prisons. This interest is reflected in the Summer 1994 issue of *New Directions for Institutional Research,* edited by a vice-chancellor and a director of institutional research at Indiana–Purdue University in Indianapolis. A long checklist of service-quality indicators appears at the volume's end (Bottrill & Borden, 1994, pp. 107–119). Six of them relate to the library and are measures new to most academic librarians:

- Percentage of courses requiring students to use the library for research projects;
- Number of items checked out of the library by undergraduates;
- Number of library computer searches initiated by undergraduates;

- Percentage of library study spaces occupied by students;
- Number of pages photocopied by students; and
- Percentage of students completing their first year without checking out a library book.

These items measure the impact or the penetration of the library into the lives of the students; they do not inherently measure service quality. However, as baseline measures of use, they are more than most libraries have now. Based on these indicators, a library's rating will be influenced by students' past experiences using the library: Positive experiences are repeated and negative ones are avoided. Furthermore, the experiences of former and current students create a reputation for the library that will influence the behavior of new students.

Astin (1985) offered four ways of looking at excellence in higher education: excellence as reputation, excellence as resources, excellence as outcomes, and excellence as content. However, he recommended that educational institutions focus on "talent development" to enhance students' knowledge and personal development, and on faculty members' scholarly pedagogical ability and productivity (p. 61). Some institutions have begun to concern themselves with the quality of the educational product, and several institutions now give limited warranties either to graduates or to their employers. Additional courses are offered to recent graduates of some teacher training programs whose school districts are unsatisfied with their performance; others offer free courses to their graduates unable to find employment after a certain period of time.

Because the cost of tuition has spiralled upward since the 1980s and the competition for students has intensified, higher education has become greatly interested in marketing. The introduction of two new journals supports this premise: The *Journal of Marketing for Higher Education,* which carries articles on customer service, and the *Journal of Customer Services in Marketing and Management,* which contains articles on higher education. The intent of marketing, of course, is to attract more students.

Currently all segments of higher education seek ways to enhance revenue. The possibility of the library offering information services for a fee to businesses was recently mentioned by the president of a private university as a way to produce revenue for the institution.

THE NATURE OF SERVICES

Every librarian knows the quality of customer services cannot be measured in the same way as the quality of a tangible item, such as a toaster, can be assessed. LoSardo and Rossi (1993) outlined some frustrating and frequently overlooked aspects of service provision:

- ➥ "Services are highly variable" because they are "subject to the whims and unpredictability" of the employee providing the service.
- ➥ Customers also display the same variability as the staff. Customers can be "maddeningly imprecise or assign different meanings to the same request."
- ➥ Services are transient in that "they are produced for and immediately consumed by the customer."
- ➥ "[S]ervices can't be produced in advance and stockpiled....There is a finite time period...in which...[the provider] can offer...service or else lose the opportunity and the customer." (pp. 46–47)

Nevertheless, service quality can be measured as demonstrated by Federal Express, a delivery company with 90,000 employees in 127 countries. Federal Express expects that *every* package its employees handle be delivered by the time promised or the sender's money is refunded. The first service company to win the Malcolm Baldrige National Quality Award,[1] Federal Express has identified 12 factors that cause customer dissatisfaction and are, therefore, indicators of unsatisfactory performance. A number of demerits are associated with each of the 12 based on that factor's severity in the eyes of customers and the company. (For example, the loss of a package earns the greatest number of demerits.) (*Blueprints for Service Quality*, 1991). Federal Express totals up its demerits and calculates its score *every day*. On its best day ever it achieved 99.7% in quality performance. The company continues to strive for improvement to achieve its service goal of 100% every day ("Not Resting on Its Laurels," 1994).

Harvey Mackay (1995), president of a stationery company and author of *Swim with the Sharks without Being Eaten Alive* and *Sharkproof,* said, "Outfits that don't have to provide quality don't. That's why 'accidents' will happen" (p. E6). In one of his syndicated newspaper columns entitled "Hospitals Could Learn Plenty from Market-Oriented Firms," he cited medical horror stories—one concerning a women who died from overdoses of chemotherapy, and another about a man whose "good" leg was amputated by mistake. The hospitals responded that their intentions were good!

THE CONCEPT OF QUALITY SERVICE

Quality is in the eyes of the beholder, and although it sounds like a cliché, it

---

[1] In 1987, Congress authorized the Malcom Baldrige National Quality Award to reward quality achievement and excellence in business.

is literally true. If customers say there is quality service, then there is. If they do not, then there is not. It does not matter what an organization believes about its level of service.

Greyhound Lines, the bus company, wants new employees to understand service quality (or, more appropriately, the lack of it) from the customers' perspectives. Greyhound requires new employees to experience "reality training" by riding on buses that are dirty and smelly. They are made to wait in long lines and then treated indifferently and rudely. "One month after reality training began, Greyhound realized a 50% decrease in customer complaints," even though it had not "changed any procedures for dealing with service failures" ("Walking in Your Customers' Shoes," 1995, p. 16).

Accordingly, it is easy to understand what most people want when they go to the library. They want to identify materials pertinent to their needs. They want to locate them easily. If they want photocopies, they expect that the photocopy machines will work properly. If they have questions about how to identify materials or locate specific information, they expect staff to help them promptly and courteously. They want a quiet place to read or to study. In other words, they want what they want when they want it. They do not want the opposites of service quality: rudeness, delays, and being ignored or sent from service area to service area.

This is pretty pedestrian stuff for librarians conditioned to think their services expand intellectual horizons, and many of them do. However, if the materials are not available, if there are no quiet places to study, and if staff members are not helpful, then no higher order outcomes (such as the enhancement of learning, the facilitation of research, or the impact on intellects) will occur. The basics of service quality must be in place for any higher level library contributions to take place. "Access" is the first step in service, and "access" means obtaining materials that contain information.

FOCUS ON THE CUSTOMER

Readers, users, patrons, borrowers, and clients—all these words have been used to describe the people who come into libraries. "All of those terms are either too passive or too supply-led," meaning they are determined by the library (Barter, 1994, p. 6). Barter quoted a wonderful observation from Bob McKee's *Planning Library Service*: "A customer is someone who chooses to use a particular service or product rather than doing something else. Libraries are only used by people who choose them" (p. 6).

The idea that customers really do not know what they want and cannot properly evaluate the service is unfortunately rather widespread in the library profession. Supporters of this view cite instances of customers receiving incorrect answers to reference questions and going away satisfied because they did not know the answers were wrong. Of course they were satisfied—they asked questions of presumably knowledgeable professionals. They got answers. Not unreasonably, they believed them to be correct. That they were wrong certainly was not the customers' fault. How happy, and how willing to return, will these customers be when they find out they were given wrong answers?

Many librarians consider customers poor judges of the quality of information services (i.e., they cannot judge whether the answers are right or wrong). That may be true, but it misses the point. Any service transaction is both "process" and "outcome" (LoSardo & Rossi, 1993). The process is the way the customer is treated by the service provider, and includes factors such as courtesy, clear communication, and attention to the customer's request. What the customer thinks about *both* the process and the outcome of the service is the important issue in customers' perceptions.

Who has a better mental construct of service quality than the customers? These constructs are modified or reinforced by every transaction (the combination of process and outcome) between the library and its customers. Ultimately it is the customer who decides whether the service has value by weighing the results obtained against the cost involved in effecting the transaction. Cost can include time, frustration, annoyance, or effort. It also includes the literal cost of getting to the library, which for many people means money. How the cost equates with the perceived benefits of the service determines whether or not customers will return to the library. Customers evaluate the service, and its component parts, either positively or negatively every time they come to the library and make decisions about continued use based on past experiences. It is important to understand that customers are continually assessing the library because the marketing literature states again and again that it is easier to keep customers than to get new ones. The reputation of the library is enhanced or diminished not only in the eyes of its customers, but in the minds of those with whom customers discuss interactions with the library.

Libraries cannot satisfy every request for information or every search for a book, but that does not mean they cannot try to improve. Like everyone else, librarians expect:

- Pharmacists to have the medicine to fill their prescriptions, and to fill them correctly;
- Banks to keep their deposits and withdrawals perfectly;
- Airlines to get them to their destinations safely and without undue delay; and
- Their accountants to do their tax forms well enough to keep them out of trouble with the Internal Revenue Service.

Why should the librarians' customers expect anything less?

ARE STUDENTS REALLY CUSTOMERS?

Thinking of library users as customers is a new concept for many librarians. However, said Sirkin (1993), "The 'customer' problems of libraries have more in common with the 'customer' problems of other businesses than librarians like to think" (p. 72), and, as Shapiro and Long (1994) wrote, "Much like the business sector, we in academic libraries are pre-occupied with the future and our ability to maintain our market share and to prosper" (p. 285). However, most academic librarians have a hard time thinking of people—especially students—who come to the library as customers, even though:

> Students are the only ones who can furnish a view of what our colleges or universities look like from the receiver's perspective. What do our students think about our programs and services? How can their thoughts be used in improving educational and administrative services? These are simple questions, yet often ignored. (Bogue & Saunders, 1992, p. 95)

Seymour (1995) said, "Students act more like well-mannered employees than well-informed customers" (p. 20). He contended that student silence about bad or indifferent service encourages the organization's staff to look upward for approval or criticism (toward administration) rather than outward to the customers, thereby reinforcing the status quo.

The traditional attitude of the library staff has been that students should not request help beyond general directions; students should do "their own work" and learn to use the library as part of their educational development. For many students, this attitude is tantamount to throwing them in deep water without consideration of their ability to swim. Faculty are presumed to be sufficiently knowledgeable to fend for themselves, so they, too, are benignly neglected. In fact, the trend currently popular among academic librarians is to "empower the user," which seems to mean that users are on their own. However, if the user is to be self-sufficient, the system and each of its constituent parts must function effectively—a condition that few, if any, academic libraries can even define, let alone verify or achieve.

EVERYONE WORKS IN CUSTOMER SERVICE

A new idea in most libraries is that all units of the organization exist to serve customers, and all employees are service providers. However, some customers to be served are internal. For example, technical service departments have as customers public service units such as reference, circulation, and branch libraries, but few of these "behind the scenes" units consider themselves as internal suppliers to internal customers. Hinton and Schaeffer (1994) related an instance when an internal customer was attempting to get service from another unit. The supplier asked the internal customer what he liked least about dealing with the unit. The answer was, "You are arrogant" (p. 78). The internal supplier realized how easy it is for the sole providers of a service to become arrogant. "Ultimately, this arrogant attitude filters across the organization and becomes visible to external customers" (p. 79).

This relationship requires that expectations of internal customers be managed in a manner similar to those of external customers. It may be unnecessary for internal providers to educate their internal customers to the extent that public service departments educate their external customers, but internal providers should be equally as responsive to their customers' wants. When service providers understand their unit's contribution to internal customers they better comprehend the value they add to the provision of service quality. *Added value* is the measure of contribution, rather than a simple description of what the unit does (LoSardo & Rossi, 1993).

BARRIERS TO CUSTOMER SERVICE

It merits mention that:

> Non-profit organizations that are focused on themselves rather than their customers display certain characteristics. They see their services as inherently desirable, blame customer ignorance or lack of motivation when their services are not used, relegate research about customers to a minor role... and assume that they have no generic competition. With this dichotomy in use, it is easy to see how some libraries could be considered near-sighted and organization centered rather than customer centered. (Johnson, 1995, p. 323, paraphrasing Kotler & Anderson, 1991)

A major barrier to providing and assessing service quality in libraries is the profession's failure to agree on what constitutes service quality. At an Allerton Park Institute on Evaluating Service, Childers (1991), a reference service expert, stated:

> In many years of working with reference librarians, this author has been impressed by a marked lack of clarity in the policies governing reference services, especially those policies that define precisely what is to be delivered to the client...there is reason to believe that individual libraries cannot operate at optimum effectiveness or efficiency without...defin[ing] what business they are in. (p. 35)

Just as there is no consensus about reference standards, there is, likewise, no consensus about the acceptable ratio of specific authors, titles, or subjects sought by customers in relation to those works available for immediate checkout.

Perhaps academic libraries have not felt the need to set any standards for service because theirs is a captive audience. Perhaps the captive audience is the reason that the words "superior," "quality," or "best" seldom appear in library mission statements, as they do in the mission statements of such companies as Federal Express and McDonald's. Perhaps words such as "best" or "superior" are not used in library mission statements because the library intends to do good; therefore, the staff presumes that what it does is good.

Two recent publications confirm that customer service has not been a high priority for academic librarians. One is a 1994 monograph on training library staff. It contains five major sections covering "Staff Training and Orientation," "Automation Training," "Retraining, Staff Development," and "Networks and Electronic Access." Training the staff to interact with library customers is not mentioned (Glogowski, 1994). The other publication is an annotated bibliography of 1,662 items devoted solely to articles and books about academic libraries published between 1990 and 1993 (Karp, 1994). The words "customers," "patrons," and "users" are absent from the index, as is the term "service quality." There are five entries under the heading "Evaluation of Academic Libraries," but only two relate to service. Because the concept of service has a low priority, it is not surprising that librarians have failed to establish any criteria by which to assess whether service is good or poor.

Organizational rigidity is another barrier to customer service. Tradition, practices gradually accumulated to form service patterns, and biased interpretations go unnoticed and unchallenged and become part of the organization's "core behavior" (Hinton & Schaeffer, 1994, p. 88). However, because service traditionally has been departmentalized:

> People who are not in contact with customers tend to focus inward [and] concentrate on their own projects or goals.... They often have no idea how their company's products or services are used by their customers... They are not connected in any meaningful way to their customers. (Disend, 1991, p. 32)

Service merits only lip service in some libraries because it is clear that the organization comes first: The most important people to please are the administrators and unit managers, followed by the employees. Customers are libraries' last consideration. Good customer service has no place in the reward system, especially in the many organizations that emphasize publications and professional activities as desirable staff activities at the expense of customer service. Putting the lowest paid, least skilled people out front to serve the public clearly proclaims the low priority of customer service.

Cohesiveness, the sense that everyone is working toward the same goal of quality service, is commonly lacking. "Our preoccupation with internal matters, with form rather than substance and individualism rather than teamwork are the major threats to our collective success and our libraries' effectiveness" (Shaughnessy, 1995, p. 157). Or, as Disend (1991) said, "When organizations are focused on internal issues instead of concentrating on satisfying customers, it often leads to a 'what's best for me' mentality, turf protecting, internal politics… excessive rules, and bureaucracy" (p. 29).

One excuse that librarians give for not thinking of people in the library as customers is that no money changes hands the way it does in a bookstore. We have heard librarians say that they should not be expected to respond to the public like employees in commercial establishments because their service is free. This is both erroneous and dangerous. It is erroneous because most funding for academic libraries comes from tuition or taxes. Consider the academic library with an annual budget of $12 million in a university with 1,000 full-time faculty and 24,000 students. One could say the annual cost of the library per capita for faculty and students for the year is $480, because that $12 million could have been applied either to faculty raises or to tuition reduction. (Would students at your college or university agree library service is worth the cost?) Failure to respond to customers is dangerous because new technology, especially electronic access to commercial document delivery services and the Internet, has freed the formerly captive audience to explore other ways of obtaining information needed for work and study. The number of electronic resources available to everyone with a computer and a modem will continue to grow dramatically.

Also, library services may come to be perceived as irrelevant for on-campus courses as institutions get more involved in distance education delivered directly into students' homes via television and/or the Internet and the "franchising" of courses to other schools. (Both methods are aimed at enhancing revenue.) One way that librarians can respond is by stressing customer service in the delivery of information. They must recognize that service responsive to customer expectations and needs is becoming increasingly crucial to the well-being of their institution because customers have an ever-widening range of choices in terms of getting what they want when they want it.

As the notion of collection changes with the impact of electronic delivery of both bibliographic and full-text information, "The process of increased focus on customers comes to include designing technical interfaces, managing on-site and virtual library operations, hiring consultative personnel, and many other aspects of library and community development" (Johnson, 1995, p. 319).

EXPECTATIONS ON BOTH SIDES

Libraries expect a lot from the people who come in. They expect them to know how to use a catalog (online, microfilm, or card) or an index (printed, online, CD-ROM, or on film). They expect them to know how to interpret classification numbers and/or indexing abbreviations, and to know how they are used to find things in the stacks, sometimes in a building with 8 or 10 floors. Should the materials sought not be in their proper places, the library metaphorically shrugs: So sorry.

Librarians seem largely unaware that users, especially first-time ones, are not privy to the messages conveyed in library jargon, or to idiosyncracies of classification and signage peculiar to an institution's internally nurtured customs. Libraries expect users not only to understand that current periodicals are not to be found with the bound copies, but also to know that "periodicals" and "serials" are librarians' words for magazines, and to be able to discern whether the library shelves the magazines with the books or shelves them in a separate place. Libraries expect users to be aware that back issues of newspapers and selected magazines are kept in micro format, and they may expect that users will, unassisted, retrieve the correct roll of film or fiche and insert it perfectly into the appropriate machine. Libraries expect users to know that government documents are classified differently and kept separately from "regular" books.

In contrast, library users, especially unsophisticated ones, expect to be treated like customers, the way they are treated in commercial establishments. A vice-president of Educom, an association that promotes the use of technology in higher education, in discussing the changing demographic nature of students who are older, female, primarily part-time and nonresidential said:

> Adult students are more likely to define quality in the language of the quality improvement movement, namely, satisfaction of customer needs, than in the traditional measures of quality used in higher education, namely, rich resources as represented by the size of libraries, staff-to-student ratios, and number and size of grants and contracts won by faculty. Adult students look for increased competition between higher education providers to work to their advantage as consumers. (Twigg, 1994, p. 24)

In other words, adult students want the library to work for them. They want it to be open at times convenient for them. They expect to find the item or the information they want without a hassle. When they ask a question relating to information sources, they expect that the answers given will be complete and correct, and they expect to be treated in a reasonably prompt and courteous manner by a knowledgeable staff. The library's degree of success in meeting customer expectations should be the focus of its quality assessment; customers care nothing about the way the library's budget, volumes, or staff size compare with those of some other institution.

The funders represent another constituency that must be satisfied with the library's quality. Administrators in higher education fund the library on the premise that it facilitates the education of the students and the research of the faculty. No research has tested whether the library actually succeeds in accomplishing this joint mission. What little research has been done indicates that the percentage of courses using the reserve room for required readings is slight (Rambler, 1982). In times of shrinking financial resources, when legislators are skeptical about faculty workloads and courses they dismiss as "trendy," higher education administrators are looking for ways to prove that funds are wisely spent.

WHAT IS IMPORTANT TO CUSTOMERS VERSUS
WHAT IS IMPORTANT TO LIBRARIANS

A number of studies have attempted to grapple with the question of effectiveness or performance measures for libraries. One of the most recent was conducted by McDonald and Micikas (1994) who administered a 95-item questionnaire to librarians working in colleges and universities in the Middle Atlantic states. The librarians were asked to rank the "relative importance" of their activities or the influence of the library. All the items allowed a response based on a 7-point scale, thus ensuring some comparability between statements. Any item receiving a median score of 4 or higher indicated a topic of some importance to these librarians.

The most important items in terms of rankings by median scores are:

1. Librarians provide informal guidance in the use of the library and its materials. (6.295)
2. Wherever available, [the library] provides full MARC cataloging for library materials. (6.159)
3. [Most] staff members, in positions which this library considers professional, have master's degrees in library and information science from a school accredited by the American Library Association. (6.157)
4. Library staff provide prompt, courteous, and consistently reliable services. (6.042)
5. Librarians are involved in formal efforts to teach students information-seeking skills. (5.992)
6. The library is responsive to the requirements of the college's educational programs and curricula. (5.945)
7. The library maintains a formal and well-publicized interlibrary

    loan service. (5.860)

8. Librarians understand and support the mission and goals of the college. (5.792)

9. The library provides sufficient indexing and abstracting materials to enable the user to identify most of the materials required to meet his information needs regardless of its location on or off campus. (5.726)

Curiously, the lowest score, 2.474, was for the statement "Students are consistently involved in the selection of library materials." Clearly, the librarians queried in this study did not consider customer elements as important as MARC records, which was ranked second in importance.

Van House and Childers (1993) compared the opinions of seven different groups including trustees, government officials, library administrators, library staff, and users on the importance of 62 service factors such as hours of operation and friendliness of staff. Although they found that the choices of each group were more similar than dissimilar, there were also some significant relationship patterns. The choices of library users correlated most closely with those of community leaders (0.86), local officials (0.80), and Friends groups (0.88) and had the lowest correlation with the choices of library managers (0.57), library staff (0.58) and library trustees (0.65), where 1.0 would be perfect agreement. In other words, those outside the library view things very differently than those inside.

For the sake of survival, the insiders had better get "Close to the Customer." That was Peters and Waterman's (1982) mantra for the secret of successful businesses in their bestseller, *In Search of Excellence*. The concept remains valid. Clearly, librarians need to heed these words and work with customers to enhance service quality, especially because in the next few years both academic libraries and higher education will experience great change as a result of the increasing emphasis on information technology and decreasing emphasis on the campus and on the library as a physical place.

Chapter 2

Evaluation

Library researchers and managers alike have questioned the ability of users to evaluate the services, collections and staff, emphasizing the inclination of users to report strong positively biased answers irrespective of the quality of information received.

Moving away from this perspective, more researchers and managers are beginning to accept the premise "that as the ultimate consumer of the outputs, the user is likely to be the most qualified to evaluate the quality of the... service [received]."

—Dalton, 1992, p. 89

E valuation is the process of identifying and collecting data about an organization or its specific programs, operations, and/or services. These data, viewed within a decision-making or policy-setting context, provide insights into the effectiveness, efficiency, impact, and value of a program, operation, or service; the data also provide a basis for making recommendations for improvements. In effect, decision makers view evaluation as a means to gain information useful in deciding whether to continue a program, service, or activity; in improving practices and procedures; in crafting program strategies and techniques; in instituting similar programs elsewhere; in allocating resources among competing programs or services; and in ensuring that the organization is responsive to the information needs and information-gathering preferences of their clientele. Evaluation, which "consists of comparing 'what is' with 'what ought to be'" (Van House, Weil, & McClure, 1990, p. 3), incorporates planning, research, and change; ongoing evaluation is integral to the maintenance of a dynamic, effective, and efficient organization in tune with its clientele.

Evaluation supports a number of organizational and administrative activities. Many of these activities (e.g., decision making, needs assessment, development of goals and objectives, marketing, and communication) are essential planning ingredients. Effective planning is impossible without an evaluation component, and evaluation has little practical utility unless its findings are integrated into the planning process.

The concept of measurement is closely related to evaluation; however, while measurement may lead to evaluation and evaluation may require measurement, the two processes differ. Measurement is the process of assigning numbers to describe or represent some object or phenomenon in a standardized manner (see Boyce, Meadow, & Kraft, 1994, pp. 3–5). Evaluation, which may include the measurement process, adds components of the research process, planning, and implementation strategies to change or improve the organization or a specific activity.[1]

As Hernon and McClure (1990) reminded us:

> Evaluation embraces change and encourages libraries to treat change as a positive force. By engaging in planning and research, librarians have a better idea of the future and they can meet that future with relevant, effective, and efficient services and activities. Furthermore, they can meet new challenges and innovations, and libraries will continue to play an important and positive role in the information society. (pp. 238–239)

OBSTACLES TO EVALUATION

The most detrimental obstacles are the unfounded beliefs that "everything is fine in my organization or department" and that "we intuitively know what our customers want and need, and the extent to which they are satisfied with the programs and services provided." Faith in common-sense and intuitive approaches to organizational effectiveness is simple-minded and unrealistic given present-day conditions related to the management of complex organizations, innovative technologies, and limited resources.

In the vast majority of instances, managers simply do not know how well library programs, services, and activities meet the information needs and preferences of customers. Managers have not allowed themselves to know if specific services and programs are effective and efficient, if customers consider these programs and services of high quality, or if resources could be better spent on supporting different activities, programs, and services.

Evaluation-related obstacles occur when the findings of an evaluation

---

[1] See Chapters 2 and 4 of Hernon and McClure (1990) for a discussion of the phases and steps of the evaluation process.

study are inappropriately applied or used merely to serve organizational or administrative self-interests (Suchman, 1972, p. 81). For example, evaluation might be misused to:

- Justify a weak or bad program by deliberately evaluating only those aspects that look good on the surface. Appearance replaces reality;
- Cover up program failure or errors by avoiding objective appraisal. Vindication replaces verification;
- Torpedo or destroy a program regardless of its effectiveness or quality. Politics replaces research;
- Conduct evaluation to give the appearance of objectivity or professionalism. Ritual replaces research; and
- Delay needed action by pretending to seek out facts. Research replaces decision making.

The evaluation process could be subverted by staff anxious to mislead a manager, decision maker, or a governing body. Under such circumstances, evaluation is a waste of time, personnel, and other resources. Furthermore, it damages the credibility of the organization and the morale of the organization's staff.

In some instances, there is a real fear that evaluation might indicate that a program or service is ineffective, inefficient, or of low or mediocre quality. Evaluation may reveal that existing resources are being wasted on activities that do not fulfill customers' information needs, or show that staff members are unable to perform their responsibilities effectively and efficiently.

The fact that many librarians are inadequately trained to conduct evaluation research is another obstacle to successful evaluation. Furthermore, evaluation studies are often complex to develop and implement and may require the use of sophisticated research designs and complex statistical procedures that go beyond basic descriptive statistics (see Hernon, 1994b, Chapter 5).

Other obstacles to successful evaluation include the perceived lack of resources to support the evaluation process, and the unwillingness or inability of decision makers to implement the recommendations upon the study's completion. These obstacles should not be allowed to become an unyielding block to positive change in the library. Library managers who want to establish meaningful programs of evaluation can do it. The only requirements are: (a) a commitment to evaluation; (b) basic planning and evaluation skills and competencies; (c) an understanding of fundamental research and statistical processes; and (d) recognition that an evaluation study must be done if the organization is to meet its mission, goals, and objectives in an effective, efficient, and high quality manner. The key steps are to identify what information is needed, how best to gather and interpret it, and how to implement positive change.

ACCOUNTABILITY

Because it is so difficult to control the outcome of research in many situations, image protectors and image inflators probably would prefer not to engage in evaluation. They would rather rely merely on perceptions and subjective impressions. Even in a dynamic organization, decision makers might want to monitor carefully a proposed evaluation study to determine the extent to which its findings will challenge the organization's image and expectations. However, having and applying information and data to decision making become a form of organizational power that gives decision makers a competitive edge in supporting change or the status quo. Information can enable an organization to advance a dynamic image and role as well as meet its mission, goals, and objectives. Evaluators with an unbiased interest in the outcome of findings would be reluctant to conduct studies in a repressive or restrictive environment. Evaluation, after all, is most productive in an open organization truly interested in planning and self-improvement, and in demonstrating its *worth* and *value*.

Although there are many reasons for not conducting evaluation studies and for not engaging in planning, effective and efficient management requires both planning and evaluation. The expectation that more organizations will rely on data rather than testimonials to justify their budgets and operating expenses underscores the importance of planning and evaluation. The trend toward holding organizations accountable indicates that the pressure to engage in planning and evaluation originates externally and may be an important impetus to gather information and data addressing specific needs of the organization. Librarians can use such information and data to improve and justify decisions made in response to meeting the information needs of their customers. As McDonald and Micikas (1994) note:

> A fundamental objective of assessment is to know where one is, to be sure that one is travelling in the right direction. It is during periods of change and transition, perhaps, when organizations (and their constituents) need most to be sure that they are effective ones, especially if they wish to remain in charge of that change.[2] (p. 119)

---

[2] "In the evolving information and instructional environment on campus, the question is not whether libraries will change. Rather the issue is how libraries will change and how they will be recognized as effective ones during, perhaps, a protracted period of transition. And just as importantly, how will they subsequently measure their effectiveness as organizations different from earlier classic academic libraries and needing to employ criteria on which there may not be wide 'professional' consensus?" (McDonald & Micikas, 1994, p. 119)

EVALUATION CONCEPTS

Evaluation involves five measurement concepts. They are:

- *Extensiveness* is the amount of service provided in relation to the size of the population served. This criterion is generally a measure of quantity.
- *Effectiveness,* a multidimensional construct requiring the use of multiple measures, frequently examines the extent to which organizational goals and objectives are met.
- *Efficiency* is the economy and appropriateness of resource allocations.[3]
- *Costing* (cost-effectiveness or cost-benefit) views the cost of providing a program, service, or activity in relationship to either stated goals and objectives, or the benefits derived from that program, service, or activity.[4]
- *Quality,* which in the literature of library and information science has frequently been equated with effectiveness. However, it assumes other meanings in other literatures (see Chapter 3).

Traditionally, libraries have concentrated on efficiency criteria: for instance, the number of items cataloged per day, or the number of reference transactions completed per week. Effectiveness can be assessed from a number of viewpoints ranging from that of the individual program, service, or activity to the common perspective of the entire organization. Effectiveness studies view quality from the institution's perspective, but quality has another, unique perspective—that of the customer. In effect, as Childers and Van House (1993), note:

> For the library manager, effectiveness is not only a matter of running an effective organization. It is equally a matter of *representing* the library's effectiveness to key stakeholders—that is, *assessing* the library and *communicating* that assessment. Representing it well means the manager has to identify the key stakeholders in the library's future, determine their priorities, and decide how to speak to them. (p. 8)

We would not disagree with this characterization. However, it is only half the

---

[3] Wilson (1995) views efficiency from another perspective, that of relevant information: finding "too late" information that "would make a difference," or the extent to which all available relevant information is used. The latter instance stands in sharp contrast to another "kind of nonuse of information: nonuse because of failure to find." (p. 46)

[4] The difference between a cost-effectiveness and a cost-benefit study is that the former compares costs to the actual impact of a service, program, or activity, and the latter requires the assignment of a monetary value to that service, program, or activity.

picture; this book presents another part of that picture.

Confusion between effectiveness and efficiency results in the following:

- Doing things well (efficiency) that do not need to be done (ineffectiveness).
- Constantly striving to gather more resources as an end unto themselves—with limited consideration of the degree to which the resources are accessible and meet the information needs of customers. The assumption is that bigger collections automatically mean better service to users.
- Inability to describe how well services are performed.
- Failure to identify specific priorities for library programs, services, and activities. As a result, librarians might believe that the library can provide all information services to all constituencies all the time.

To disregard the need to evaluate is to continue programs, services, and activities that are ineffective, inefficient, or both. Such disregard may also result in the failure to set priorities and to improve mediocre or inferior programs or services; the inability to demonstrate the excellence of high quality programs, services, and activities to institutional administrators and outside agencies; and so forth.

The Public Library Effectiveness Study, which contributed to the understanding of how library effectiveness may be measured, identified indicators of effectiveness for public libraries. It grouped these indicators into eight "sets, or dimensions, of effectiveness" (Childers & Van House, 1993):

- Counts of library activity;
- Internal processes;
- Community fit;
- Access to materials;
- Physical facilities;
- Boundary spanning;
- Service offerings; and
- Service to special groups.

Each set consists of "subordinate indicators" (p. 29). Thus, it is possible to view sets or dimensions for different approaches to organizational effectiveness (see the section of this book on "Typical Approaches toward Gauging Organizational Effectiveness"). The goals-and-objective approach need not be the dominate one. Furthermore, researchers can explore the sets in other types of libraries and pursue the question "Are there differences among constituent groups in their preferences among indicators, dimensions, and/or definitions of library effectiveness?" (see Calvert & Cullen, 1994).

The efficiency of a program, service, or activity cannot be improved past a certain critical point without injuring its effectiveness and vice-versa. Thus, continued attention to increasing efficiency may become counterproductive to effectiveness. For example, having reference staff drastically increase the number of transactions completed (efficiency) will reach a point after which transactions will no longer be answered correctly (ineffectiveness) because of the overload of work. Effectiveness, as typically reported in the literature of library and information science, views quality from an institutional, not a customer, perspective. Because quality is multi-faceted, it should not be seen merely as a component of effectiveness. Clearly, quality is a dimension of its own.

This chapter will review key concepts and show that librarians wishing to engage in evaluation can select from many different vantage points. This book presents librarians with an alternative perspective, and encourages them to review their data collection priorities and to select evaluation efforts that improve the organization's ability to better serve its customers. This book also encourages librarians to view evaluation from the customers' perspective and offers a base upon which researchers can build.

EFFECTIVENESS

McDonald and Micikas (1994), to some extent, adopted and adapted the work of Kim Cameron, an expert on organizational effectiveness. Cameron concluded the effectiveness of colleges and universities (and presumably their libraries) depends on multidimensional and multivariate measures for assessment. Another Cameron concept is that effectiveness is a mental construct inferred from an organization's behavior, and not observed directly. Because individuals form their own impressions, consensus on any single model of effectiveness is unlikely. However, "an organization's effectiveness is based on the conception its members have of that organization" (p. 2). Cameron defined effectiveness as "successful organizational transactions." These transactions include "the interaction among all activities and people in the library, as well as those transactions between the library and its environment" (p. 31). Finally, effective organizations generate valued and desired outcomes—"those outcomes to which the external environment is receptive or which it considers important" (p. 36).

In *Academic Libraries,* McDonald and Micikas (1994) examined three research questions:

➥ Is it possible to establish criteria for assessing academic library organizational effectiveness and to develop an instrument that will measure library effectiveness?

- Can dimensions of academic library organizational effectiveness be identified?
- Can groups of academic libraries be identified that show high effectiveness in contrast with others that indicate lower effectiveness?

They conclude that they can answer each question, but they concede that "less effective libraries may have been unwilling to respond and thus, the data may be biased in favor of the more effective ones" (p. 78). They further caution about the possibility of individual and library bias reflecting perceptions at odds with reality. Aggregating the data and, thereby:

> Reducing the number of variables to a manageable level requires the research to rely on chance more than might be justified... [and] it is possible that some of the relationships reported are the result of statistical procedures rather than actual relationships. (p. 85)

McDonald and Micikas provided an excellent summary of the research on library effectiveness and offer theoretical insights into organizational effectiveness. They also recognized the importance of gauging the effectiveness of both individual units within the organization and the entire organization itself. Nonetheless, their model for assessing academic library effectiveness remains elusive; they did not follow through on Cameron's significant ideas such as successful organizational transactions and the valued outcomes.

The quest for the "Grail of Library Goodness" (McDonald & Micikas, 1994, p. 87) considers service quality superficially through a few questions such as "the library's cataloging system is easily understood and used by faculty and students" (p. 134) and "the library staff provide prompt, courteous, and consistently reliable service" (p. 126). Both examples contain multiple concepts; putting two or more ideas in the same statement may cause confusion because the responses to multiple ideas may not be clearly interpreted. This approach is symptomatic of a tendency to view quality as a subset of effectiveness, as frequently occurs in works in library and information science.

TYPICAL APPROACHES TOWARD GAUGING ORGANIZATIONAL EFFECTIVENESS

"Organizations are supposed to be good; libraries are supposed to be good. The question of goodness translates in today's library management literature into the subject of *effectiveness*" (Childers & Van House, 1993, p. 5). Although there are four general approaches to viewing organizational effectiveness, the first, or goal–objective approach, is most frequently used in the evaluation of library and information center programs, services, and activities. Because this approach "sees organizations as instruments designed to achieve specific ends" (Van House & Childers, 1993, p. 1), effectiveness is measured by ascertaining the extent to which stated goals and objectives have been attained. Nonetheless, this approach has been criticized because the "official goals are not always the same as... [the] actual or real ones" (McDonald & Micikas, 1994). "Likewise, not all goals are of equal priority in theory or in practice, nor do all constituencies agree on the priorities assigned to goals." As well, the "influence of the environment on the organization and its goals is not addressed" (p. 8).

Despite the dominance of this approach in the evaluation literature of library and information science, three other approaches also have a place in evaluation. The four approaches are not contradictory, but do emphasize different aspects of the organization, its roles and performance. Moreover, like the goal approach, the other approaches have their own sets of limitations (pp. 8–11).

The second approach, which focuses on process or natural systems, "defines an organization as a collective not only seeking to achieve specific goals, but also engaged in activities required to maintain itself as a social unit" (Van House & Childers, 1993, p. 2). Thus, "effectiveness is measured by goal [and objectives] attainment, and also by internal processes and organizational health" (p. 2).

The next approach, one of an open system, "emphasizes the interdependence of the organization with its environment." An effective organization, therefore, "responds to the demands of its environment according to its dependence on the various components of the environment for resources" (p. 2).

Multiple constituencies, the final approach, "defines effectiveness as the degree to which the needs and expectations of strategic constituencies are met." These constituencies need not be the "power elite" (p. 2); simply stated, the emphasis is on determining the extent to which the priorities of various stakeholders are met.

SYSTEMS ANALYSIS

Systems analysis provides a framework for viewing organizational activities as well as visualizing and studying problems related to effectiveness and efficiency. Systems analysis becomes important when problems transcend individual departments and encompass multiple activities.

Systems analysis encourages human interaction and group communication, involving different facets of the organization to better understand common problems and seek their resolution. Individual units of the organization might focus narrowly on a problem and deal with it within narrow confines without realizing that one unit's action impacts other units. Systems analysis, therefore, stresses the larger picture and knowledge of work flow, space layout, and so forth.

Through systems analysis, organization members are persuaded to accept change. Change is any planned or unplanned alteration in the status quo affecting an organization's structure, services, programs, or allocation of resources. Both systems analysis and evaluation require that the organization be willing to live with the results of change, no matter what they are.

General systems thinking emphasizes flexibility, the environment, and the various interdependent parts of which the organization consists. A system is defined as a group of interrelated parts acting together to accomplish specific goals and objectives. One part affects not only the other parts but also the behavior of the entire system; the overall manner in which the various parts combine to affect the system is greater than their sum. In short, the interaction among the different parts of the system produces a system attribute not achievable by the individual parts alone. Systems analysis promotes better understanding of the relationship among those interdependent parts and their impact on the operation of the organization.

An open system, one that exchanges resources with the environment, contains five parts (see Figure 2.1):

- *Input.* The system deals with internal and external factors from the larger environment:
  - Internal factors, coming from within the organization, include budgeting (money), clientele, equipment, information, legal or regulatory requirements, and staffing; and
  - External factors are attributes which act upon the institution from outside. They are economic, physical, political, and social in nature.
- *Throughput* (or process). Resources are moved through the system, where they are transformed into products. Activities central to this part of the cycle include review and decision making;
- *Output.* The system sends the transformed resource (a product, service, or other kind of result) back to the environment;
- *Feedback.* The system obtains information from the environment to help it regulate the importation of resources and other system activities. Feedback among various parts of a system can occur without direct intervention with the environment; and
- *Outcome.* The output has either an internal or external impact on the environment. Internal impacts are likely to occur within a couple of years, whereas external ones take place in 5 to 10 years. External impacts include political, economic, educational, ethical,

social, and physical factors. The program or service results might be unitary or multiple, intended or unintended, positive or negative, or short or long term.

The general systems model serves as a reminder that there is a connection between inputs and outputs and that evaluation examining effectiveness might consider impacts and outcomes within the context of specific inputs (indicators of those resources essential to library services), outputs (indicators of the services resulting from library activities), goals, and objectives. An analysis of organizational activities and operations can lead to the: (a) identification of potentially significant problems requiring research that directly impact on planning and decision making; (b) evaluation of programs, services, and activities; and (c) the development of plans to ensure that the organization adopts change that will result in improved programs, services, and operations.

Other Characteristics of a System

As Nadler and Tushman (1980, pp. 271–278) discuss, other characteristics of an open system include:

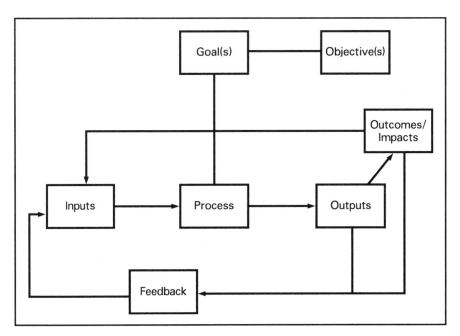

Figure 2.1. General Systems Model.

🐦 *Differentiation.* As a system grows, it tends to become more specialized, to add components, and to develop additional transformation processes and feedback loops;

🐦 *Equifinality.* The organization and processes of different systems may produce the same end result;

🐦 *Negative Entropy.* Positive entropy represents the death of the system; thus, negative entropy is obtaining adequate resources for the system to accomplish goals and objectives, to adapt to changing environments, and to support system differentiation; and

🐦 *Equilibrium Seeking.* The system tends to move toward a state where all elements successfully contribute to the organization's accomplishment of goals and objectives. When changes that result in an imbalance are made, different system components restore the balance both within the system and in terms of the system's relationship with the environment.

These four characteristics of an open system describe the typical organization. Evaluators must recognize and cope with these characteristics as well as with political factors and a bureaucracy that may favor the status quo.

In summary, the general systems model and open systems characteristics are tools for librarians considering how the various parts of the organization work (or do not work) together, the impact of specific resources on various areas of the organization, the success with which organizational resources are transformed into products and services, and how well the collection of input and output measures respond to the library's mission and the information needs of the library's clientele.

ADOPTING A USER PERSPECTIVE THROUGHOUT THE ORGANIZATION

A systems approach, as previously noted, encourages librarians to view problems and issues in the context of the entire organization. Reference service, for instance, is not isolated from activities occurring elsewhere in the organization; failure to catalog items promptly, receive items swiftly through interlibrary loan, or reshelve books with dispatch, may adversely affect the quality of reference service provided to library customers. Combining a systems approach with a customer perspective forces librarians to view evaluation in terms of the customers' views of quality, value, and preferences. Of course, libraries must balance these considerations with other factors, such as institutional mission and the ability to deliver the expected service. Nonetheless, libraries (like businesses) must readjust their service to better accommodate their customers; this may require a readjustment of organizational philosophy and the roles and priorities of staff.

Most evaluation studies in library and information science represent a one-time snapshot of one particular time, place, and situation. That single picture might be fuzzy or poorly centered on the key object, or it might fail to capture a critical point. There must be a commitment within every library to engage in continuous improvement of the entire organization: "Librarians and library managers need to collect long-term data, identify the root causes behind poor quality... service, and eliminate those causes" (Aluri, 1993, p. 225). Both the organization and its customers benefit when library managers and staff members look at the library "through the user's eyes" (St. Clair, 1993, p. 38), measuring service quality rather than "service quantity" (Sjolander & Sjolander, 1995, p. 66). Service quality offers librarians an opportunity to examine both successes and failures (e.g., Henderson, 1994–1995) and to implement procedures for attacking areas needing improvement.

PERFORMANCE MEASURES

Performance measures make up a broad managerial concept encompassing both *input* and *output* measures. Library managers and decision makers use performance measures to answer the question "How well is the library doing what it claims to be doing?" In other words, these measures characterize the extent, effectiveness, and efficiency of library programs and services.

There may be tradeoff relationships between specific performance measures: increasing the score of one measure may decrease the score on another. Because performance measures examine different components of the same system, they are presumably interdependent; changing one component of the system may affect another component. For example, higher circulation results in low shelf availability and shortening the loan period results in increased circulation.

The primary utility of a performance measure is for "internal self-diagnosis of library services and activities" (McClure, Zweizig, Van House, & Lynch, 1986, p. 51). Managers must select and use measures having value to their situation, and should not consider a particular score derived from calculating a measure as "inherently 'good' or 'bad'" (p. 51). Rather, they should interpret a score in the context of their expectations and their libraries' goals and objectives.

There are a number of problems inherent in performance measures: the numerator and denominator of a measure (e.g., number of titles circulated in comparison to the number of titles owned) may not compare like objects;[5] the

---

[5] If the library has large non-circulating collections, the ratio should compare the number of titles circulated and the number eligible for circulation.

development of measures has not kept pace with the shifting role of libraries in the electronic information age; measures are oriented toward the institution rather than the customer; data collection is entirely quantitative—performance measurement has yet to embrace qualitative data collection; and performance measures do not reflect the outcomes and impacts of the use of collections and services by library customers. In effect, performance measures become a tool for demonstrating accountability—the library's effective and efficient use of inputs and outputs as typically viewed from the perspective of the extent to which library goals and objectives are met.

Measuring Academic Library Performance (Van House, Weil, & McClure, 1990) identifies measurable areas, that is general user satisfaction, "materials availability and use," "facilities and library uses," and "information services." It also explains:

> The basic question to be asked in choosing measures to be implemented is: What difference will it make for us to have this information? Which data will be most useful for the decisions that face us? Some libraries will want to go into greater depth in specific areas: for these, each measure is followed by "Further Suggestions." (p. ii)

The manual advises libraries to select the most appropriate measures, adopt standardized procedures that permit trend data to emerge, and review the sampling frame. The longer the sampling period, the more likely the data will be widely generalizable.

Because "the library's ultimate goal may be defined as meeting its users' information needs, which is best assessed from the users' perspective" (p. 11), the manual includes user-oriented objective and subjective measures; however, as a result of its failure to address the role of case studies and qualitative research, the manual does not effectively capture the human element.

The forms provided by the manual are a good example of this shortcoming; despite the fact that both forms and procedures were extensively pretested for implementation in academic libraries, certain sections, such as in the "General Satisfaction Survey" (form 1–1) and the "Reference Satisfaction Survey" (form 14–1), never adequately established a theoretical framework that would allow librarians to probe fully the concept of satisfaction, including important variables such as the understandability of the information provided and the speed of service delivery. Furthermore, the language on the forms is self-defeating in that user-friendly terminology is rejected in favor of professional jargon unfamiliar to a number of library users.[6]

Overall, although the manual attempts to focus on "the outcomes of

---

[6] Naismith and Stein (1989) offer an excellent discussion of the use of library jargon. Both forms (1–1 and 14–1) merit review within that context.

library service (the effect on one's life or work, the uses to which the information is put)" (Van House, Weil, & McClure, 1990), claiming that "outcomes cannot be measured directly, but can be measured indirectly by user satisfaction" (pp. 12–13), it is not a successful attempt when viewed in those terms. The authors do not adequately define satisfaction, and fail to place the concept in a usable framework. Most importantly, the separation between quality and effectiveness is never clearly delineated, and the discussion does not transcend the institutional realm: "Comparisons [among libraries] must be carefully considered. They can only be made in the context of the parent institutions' missions, the libraries' missions and goals, and individual constraints and environmental factors" (p. 13).

OUTCOME AND IMPACT MEASURES

Some confusion exists in the literature as to the definition of outcomes. Some authors equate outcomes with impacts, whereas others differentiate between them. This book adopts the latter approach. Outcomes deal with service quality, satisfaction, and preferences, judged only from the perspective of the library's customers (see Chapter 3). Impact delineates among uses of collections and services, examining uses and their importance to the institution, society, and so forth. In effect, impact measures "the actual impact of libraries" (Powell, 1992, p. 245) by examining:

> How a service made a difference in some other activity or situation, for example, freshmen who took a library Internet training program had, on average, a letter grade higher in their English class than those freshmen who did not take the class. (McClure, 1994, p. 3)

Impact, in effect, might measure "how students' use of libraries affects their academic performance" (Powell, 1992, p. 245).

McClure (1994) wants to link impact, and presumably outcome, measures with networks such as the Internet. He asks:

> What measurable impacts result from faculty who regularly use list-servs? Does such involvement improve teaching or research? Does it detract from teaching or research effectiveness? Do students taking courses with faculty who use networking as an instructional process learn more or better than those who do not? (p. 4)

He refers to the answers to these questions as performance measures, whereas we suggest they might be either outcome or impact measures depending on the wording of the formula and whether or not the intent is to focus on customers rather than on the organization itself. By advocating the "need for a user perspective" (p. 4), he seems to support the development of new ways of looking at things.

EXAMPLES OF EVALUATION LITERATURE

The following list, which is suggestive rather than comprehensive, includes background works that discuss both quantitative- and qualitative-based evaluation. It indicates that, within library and information science, the focus has been on the measurement of effectiveness or efficiency, but typically not within a cost framework. Outside library and information science, there is a more developed literature on cost-effectiveness and cost-benefit. Furthermore, within our profession, there has been little attention to the customer's viewpoint as reflected through an analysis of service quality and outcome measures.

SUGGESTED READINGS

Baker, Sharon L. & F. Wilfrid Lancaster. *The Measurement and Evaluation of Library Services*. Arlington, VA: Information Resources Press, 1991. (Lancaster has produced other works, as well that list research and evaluation literature from library and information science.)

Childers, Thomas A. & Nancy A. Van House. *What's Good? Describing Your Public Library's Effectiveness*. Chicago: American Library Association, 1993.

Feeney, Mary & Maureen Grieves. *The Value and Impact of Information*. London: Bowker-Saur, 1994.

Isaac, Stephen & William B. Michael. *Handbook in Research and Evaluation*. 3rd ed. San Diego, CA: EdITS, 1995.

McDonald, Joseph A. & Lynda Basney Micikas. *Academic Libraries: The Dimensions of Their Effectiveness*. Westport, CT: Greenwood Press, 1994, Chapter 2, pp. 7–19.

Rossi, Peter H. & Howard E. Freeman. *Evaluation: A Systematic Approach*. Beverly Hills, CA: Sage, 1993.

Rubin, Irene & Herbert J. Rubin. *Hearing Data: The Art of Qualitative Interviewing*. Thousand Oaks, CA: Sage, 1995

Stake, Robert E. *The Art of Case Study Research*. Thousand Oaks, CA: Sage, 1995.

Van House, Nancy A. & Thomas A. Childers. *The Public Library Effectiveness Study*. Chicago: American Library Association, 1993.

Yin, Robert K. *Case Study Research*. Newbury Park, CA: Sage, 1989.

Chapter 3

Service Quality As Reflected in the Literature

Service management is a total organizational approach that makes quality of service, as perceived by the customer, the number one driving force for the operation of the business.

—Albrecht, 1988, p. 20

This chapter examines service quality as discussed in the literatures of government, management and marketing, higher education, and library and information science, and provides the definition and beginning framework that guided the development of the remaining chapters. The book is based on the premise that a *customer-centered* focus must be adopted by the entire organization, not just front-line staff, such as reference or circulation. As the management literature indicates, businesses exist and flourish only as long as customers purchase and endorse their products, and will fail to thrive if they develop and offer products to meet unspecified future needs or meet the needs of only a few customers of today. Envision a store that many people walk by but do not visit, or browse through with no interest in most of the products and services offered.

Of course, the comparison to libraries can be extended only so far. Because academic libraries tend not to be commercially oriented, they will not go bankrupt if students and faculty ignore their collections and services. Nonetheless, librarians should ask:

- How many people whom we are supposed to serve actually use the library?
- How well do we serve present users?
- What problems do they encounter in using the library?
- Which of these problems can we resolve or should we resolve?
- How can we maintain the support of the college or university president and other key administrators, boards of regents, legislators, and others?

The presumption in addressing such questions is that meeting and *satisfying* the present customers will result in repeat business and customer *loyalty,* and provide a base from which libraries can attract new customers while better serving existing ones (see St. Clair, 1993, pp. 12–18). Library managers and the entire staff "must buy into and enthusiastically support the concept that the service is for the users" (p. 5).

The challenge in adopting a customer focus and "achieving peak performance... is how to align the philosophies, attitudes, and behaviors of... [library] staff so as to realize their individual and collective potential" (Shaughnessy, 1995, p. 155). Shaughnessy notes that a related issue "is how to overcome the inertia imposed by smugness, or by library traditions and cultures which can inhibit our 'being all that we can be'" (p. 155). Complicating matters:

> The competition for resources on our campuses, the demand for accountability, the need to demonstrate return on investment, the need to be more effective—are placing extraordinary demands on our library organizations and on the individuals who comprise them. (p. 155)

At the same time, library staff "have had to find ways of coping with enormous workloads (brought about in part by new information technologies and steadily increasing demand for services) by staffing losses, serial crises, etc." (pp. 155–156), as they demonstrate a commitment "to the highest levels of customer service" (p. 156). In effect, there is a need to redefine priorities and to change the way that libraries do things. A key question is, "How can librarians better accomplish their activities and tasks more efficiently and effectively in order to free them to assume new ones?"

THE LITERATURE

Total Quality Management (TQM) means a total commitment to a culture of customer-orientation and satisfaction. Its purpose is to ensure both customer retention and new customer growth. Before linking customer satisfaction to TQM, an organization must identify customers' perceived *wants* and *needs,* and narrow the gap between the two. TQM, if implemented effectively, can change an organization's culture (i.e., the way things are done) so there is a sense throughout the organization that the determination of customer *wants* is everyone's responsibility. The implementation of TQM can be expedited by setting quality standards, encouraging innovation, measuring results, and taking corrective action. This section discusses the literature of various disciplines relevant to service quality.

Government

In *Reinventing Government,* Osborne and Gaebler (1992) point out:

> The fact that government cannot be run just like a business does not mean it cannot become more entrepreneurial. Any institution, public or private, can be entrepreneurial.... There is a vast continuum between bureaucratic behavior and entrepreneurial behavior, and government can surely shift its position on that spectrum.(p. 22)

By extension, there is no reason libraries cannot also become more entrepreneurial. A competitive attitude can result in greater efficiency, responsiveness to customer needs, and innovation. A "results-orientation" places attention on "outcomes, not inputs" (p. 143). There are "dozens of different ways to listen to the voice of the customer," including surveys, direct contact service, focus groups, electronic mail, complaint tracking systems, and so forth (p. 177).

To accomplish the goal of reinventing government, the Clinton administration, soon after President William J. Clinton took office, initiated the National Performance Review, which resulted in Clinton issuing Executive Order 12862—"Setting Customer Service Standards"—on September 11, 1993, (see 58 *Federal Register* 48257). He directed the federal government to become "customer-driven," noting "the standard of quality for service provided to the public shall be: Customer service equal to the best in business." He defined a customer as "an individual or entity who is directly served by a department or agency" and "best in business" as "the highest quality of service delivered to customers by private organizations providing a comparable or analogous service" (*Putting Customers First,* 1994, p. 63).

Putting Customers First (1994) resulted from the presidential directive that agencies establish service standards based on customer surveys, thus providing a customer-focus benchmark against which their performance may be measured. This government publication makes an example of the famous customer service standard of Federal Express: "priority delivery by

10:30 a.m. the next business day; regular delivery by 3 p.m." (p. 1). By implementing such a standard, the customers of this company "know exactly what to expect and employees... know their mission and the measure of success." Furthermore, the company "responds to customer needs" (p. 1).

Putting Customers First "presents more than 1,500 customer service standards, representing commitments from more than 100 federal agencies" (p. 1). As a reminder that not all customers are the same, the publication identifies 10 customer groups: beneficiaries; business; the general public; law enforcement; natural resource management; the research and academic community; state, localities, and other partners; travelers, tourists, and outdoor enthusiasts; the U.S. government and federal employees; and veterans.

The publication makes an important observation:

> There is a lot more to delivering top-notch service than just wanting to and promising to. You have to organize for responsiveness and flexibility; most of the government was organized for top-down control and risk avoidance. We are changing that. You have to train and empower employees so they can deliver the results customers want; most federal employees have been trained to follow rigid rules. We are changing that. You have to design systems to please customers.... But these changes go to the very core of government. They take time. And one of the cardinal rules of customer service is never to make a promise you can't keep; if anything, promise less, then give your customer a pleasant surprise. (p. 2)

Service standards must be measurable. Federal Express, for instance, can measure how many of its customers' packages arrive on time, and the Office of Consumer Affairs within the Department of Commerce can determine the extent to which its staff treats customers—the general public—"fairly and courteously." Staff members are instructed to answer the telephone:

> on or before the third ring. You will speak to one of our staff. On the rare occasion when no one is available, you may leave a message on our answering machine and we will return your call on the same day or the next working day. (*Putting the Customers First,* 1994, p. 94)

Furthermore, the Office's staff guarantee "always" to write letters "in plain language." Consumer complaint letters are responded to "within 10 working days; as appropriate, our written responses... will provide you with additional sources of information and redress, and will include a complaint-handling fact sheet." When staff receive a telephone complaint, "We will advise you on the telephone. If a complaint specialist is not available, we will return your call by the next business day" (p. 95).

Department of Commerce (1992), which presents strategies for "effective complaint management" (p. 1), observes that "those companies with a positive philosophy and reputation for fair complaint management have a competitive edge. Effective complaint management leads to increased customer satisfaction, which, in turn, yields greater brand loyalty" (p. iv). This business guide identifies "key ingredients in effective consumer complaint management," some of which apply to libraries:

- Management commitment;
- Publicity for the system;
- Accessibility of complaint management staff;
- Promptness and courtesy of response;
- Personalized response, whenever possible;
- Simple, clear communications with consumers;
- Objectivity and flexibility in determining the proper resolution; and
- Uniform, consistent and computerized record keeping (p. 5).

The last suggestion is an intriguing one. Computerization provides a mechanism for "enabling management to monitor the efficiency and effectiveness of the complaint management system" and for "providing market research through complaint trends" (p. 6).

The guide, which recommends the complaint management system be publicized to employees and customers, concludes effective complaint management reduces "the causes for consumer complaints" (p. 7). Table 3.1 lists those points from a "complaint management checklist" applicable to libraries.

The U.S. government, in setting standards to serve customers—the American people—is attempting to identify the needs of different constituent groups, provide a level of expectation, measure the extent of its success in meeting that level, and develop a mechanism for redressing service failures or areas needing improvement. By wanting to develop rapport with their customers, some agencies expect those directly serving the public to listen, understand the information request, be knowledgeable, and work effectively and efficiently with the customer (see Lisoskie & Lisoskie, 1993). However, it must be noted that the implementation of a customer service plan will not result in the successful reinvention of government without a long-term commitment to a formal evaluation plan that produces ongoing change and, indeed, does offset service failures.

Management and Marketing

Service quality, which is a subjective concept and more of a "global judgment... attribute" or attitude toward service (Elliot, 1994), differs from, but

Table 3.1. Complaint Management Checklist [a]

In planning a system for complaint management or evaluating the one you have in place, consider the following questions:

- Does your company view consumer satisfaction as a key ingredient of total quality management?
- Do you have a systematic strategy for complaint management?
- Do you have written procedures for your complaint management system?
- Is staff throughout the company well aware of the procedures and the importance of your complaint management system?
- Does top management directly oversee your complaint handling procedures?
- Do incentives exist to reinforce staff commitment to consumer satisfaction?
- Is your complaint system easily accessible to consumers?
- Is your complaint system computerized?
- Do you publicize your complaint system to consumers? If yes, how? Printed media (posters, advertising, monthly statements, on packaging, labeling, and products)? Communications by sales personnel?
- Is your complaint system:
  - Decentralized, with each employee, branch office, or store responsible for revolving complaints?
  - Centralized in one department or location?
  - Or, a combination of both, with larger or more serious complaints resolved in a central office?
- Are you providing adequate training for your complaint management staff?
- Do you periodically survey your customers to see if they are satisfied with your complaint management system? Do you encourage feedback?
- Do you regularly review your complaint management system and make necessary improvements?
- Do you utilize your system of complaint management for more than settling individual complaints? For example, for quality control and problem prevention?
- Does your complaint system swiftly generate systematic information about causes of complaints and complaint trends? Does this data meet your management needs?
- Do you circulate to top management periodic reports of data from complaint records with suggestions for action to prevent recurring problems?
- Can you identify areas in the company where your complaint management system is having an effect? Has it been positive or negative?

[a] The questions are reprinted from Department of Commerce (1992, pp. 12–13).

is related to customer satisfaction which examines "a specific transaction" (p. 33), perceived value, and customer preferences.[1] Obviously, the information needs and the information-seeking behavior of individuals impact the understanding and application of these key concepts.

---

[1] Value refers to the interplay among price, accessibility, and quality (see Rust & Oliver, 1994; see also Rubin, 1994).

Orr (1973) discusses the difference between quality and value in information services, and Boyce, Meadow, and Kraft (1994) provide a brief introduction to the measurement of quality for an information system. They view quality as "conformity to requirements" (p. 12).

Service quality is probably "an antecedent of customer satisfaction" (Elliot, 1994, p. 34); "higher levels of service quality result in increased customer satisfaction" (p. 38). There are three measurable perspectives of customer satisfaction: interactions with employees of the organization, the services or product used, and the organization as a system. Satisfaction includes variables such as:

- Expectations met;[2]
- Price, time, and effort—willingness to pay; and
- Willingness to return to the:
  - Same employee;
  - Same service; and
  - Organization itself.

Satisfaction might focus on expectations or difficulties encountered. The purpose of such assessment is to learn from the problems and seek improvement; it is not to embarrass employees or belittle products and services. Because problems represent opportunities to take corrective action, assessment might concentrate on questions such as:

- In the last [insert time frame] did you experience any problems in the use of our services or products? Yes___ No___.
- If you answered "yes," what was the problem?
- How did our employees deal with the problem?
- Please assess the course of action they took to resolve the problem.
- Would you use our products and services again? Yes___ No___. Please explain.

The answer to the final question dealing with willingness to return or to use again is a key factor; it provides a context for evaluating the other responses.

The principles of service quality remain the same in all service organizations, whether they be stock brokerage firms, travel agencies, libraries, or so on. Organizations lacking tangible products or services have certain common characteristics. For instance, the process of providing services requires a complex and highly efficient delivery system that is time-sensitive and user

---

2 "The interaction between the expectations and actual performance is quantified as a positive or negative outcome by computing the difference (subtraction) between them. A positive disconfirmation of expectations results in a positive value (score) of user satisfaction when the actual performance meets or exceeds the expectations of the user. However, if the actual performance is lower than the expectations, a negative disconfirmation of expectations occurs to give a negative value (score) of user satisfaction (dissatisfaction). If there is no difference between the two levels reported, then satisfaction is said to be confirmed." (Dalton, 1992, p. 91)

friendly. Furthermore, "Because the client's views about the services are subjective, a performance evaluation system must be able to capture a broad range of client satisfaction information and convert this to useful statistics from which logical inferences can be drawn" (DiPrimio, 1987, pp. 9–10). Stafford (1994, pp. 18–19) proposes a generic model for improving service quality for service providers, including 10 stages that, although connected, do not simply flow from one to the other:

- Stage 1—*Management Commitment.* Management must become committed to quality improvement and communicate that commitment to employees;
- Stage 2—*Employee Commitment and Participation.* Employees must become committed to the program and participate fully in the process;
- Stage 3—*Employee Education and Training.* Employees must be taught their role in quality improvement and learn each stage of the program;
- Stage 4—*Employee Communication.* Communication channels must be established and utilized to ensure a constant and appropriate information flow between employees and management;
- Stage 5—*Internal Organization.* A quality director should be selected, and individuals should be assigned their quality improvement responsibilities;
- Stage 6—*Objective Setting.* Each employee should set personal quality improvement objectives, both qualitative and quantitative;
- Stage 7—*Assessment and Modification Processes.* An evaluation of current quality levels must be assessed, and modifications to existing procedures should be developed and implemented;
- Stage 8—*Control.* Controls should be established to ensure continued and successful change;
- Stage 9—*Integration.* The stages should be merged together to ensure a smoothly operating system; and
- Stage 10—*Continuation.* Quality improvement is a continuous process.

Organizations that are "inwardly focused" are "misdirected" (Disend, 1991, p. 27). In some instances, organizations are "product-driven or technology-driven, not customer-driven" (p. 31). Disend identifies 11 "critical areas that affect... service levels and service quality" as:

- The business, industry, or field you're in;
- Your organization;
- Your products or services;

- ◥ Your philosophy and beliefs;
- ◥ Your customers;
- ◥ Your competition;
- ◥ Your suppliers;
- ◥ Your people;
- ◥ Your systems, policies, and procedures;
- ◥ Your service orientation; and
- ◥ Your results. (p. 104)

He also compares two views of customer service, the traditional approach and the customer-focused approach. The former, for example, regards customer complaints as a "failure" and something "to be avoided" (p. 20):

Customer complaints and problems are an irritant, something to be "handled." The emphasis is often on "taking care of it" at the time, placating customers, and not making bad situations worse. Often the same problems and complaints recur because the organization does nothing to correct them. (p. 20)

In contrast, the latter approach welcomes customer complaints, learns from customers, identifies weak areas, and takes corrective action.

As Disend (1991, p. 20) explains, "The emphasis is on resolving problems to the customer's satisfaction to keep the customer. The organization often overreacts to resolve problems and maintain customer good will." Furthermore, delivery should exceed organizational promises or preconceived notions, thereby producing "a satisfaction surprise" (Whitman, 1995, p. 19). "A single disastrous satisfaction surprise can create a lasting negative impression of a service experience, regardless of the number of previous uneventful visits" (p. 37). As a result, "If you can isolate this single bad experience, and offer an immediate remedy for it, you have a good chance of totally turning around the customer's impression" (p. 37).

The literature theorizes that most employees want to offer good service but do not always know how.[3] A number of service employees do an unsatisfactory job of satisfying their customers. The literature also identifies how *successful* service companies invest in the delivery of exceptional service by training employees who are committed to providing high quality service. Jan Carlzon (1987), former president of Scandinavian Airlines, regards every encounter between a customer and an employee as a "moment of truth," in which the success or failure of the business depends on the performance of the employee.

Table 3.2 identifies four perspectives on service quality and assesses the

---

[3] A disturbing trend in higher education, in contrast, is the increase in "self-absorption" and the decline or "demise of institutional loyalty" (Shaughnessy, 1995, p. 156).

strengths and weaknesses of each, with attention focused on "meeting and/or exceeding expectations" of both internal and external organizational customers. To explore the multiple constituency perspective, evaluators need to know who the customers are, what their expectations are, and how well the organization meets those expectations. Such information allows the organization to focus on areas needing attention, and measure progress consistently and in a timely manner. In effect, quality is a commitment to continuous improvement (see Figure 3.1).

Freemantle (1993) identifies 14 "tests for incredible customer service," including, for instance:

- Keeping the service promise;
- Five minute maximum waiting time;
- Positive employee attitudes;
- Proactive employee attitudes;

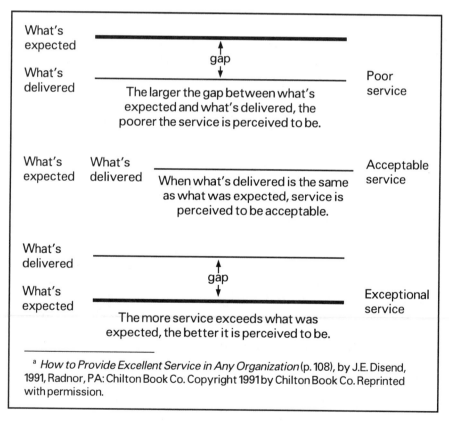

a *How to Provide Excellent Service in Any Organization* (p. 108), by J.E. Disend, 1991, Radnor, PA: Chilton Book Co. Copyright 1991 by Chilton Book Co. Reprinted with permission.

Figure 3.1. How Perceptions and Expectations Affect the Quality of Service a

Table 3.2. Perspectives of Service Quality: Their Strengths and Weaknesses [a]

Perspective	Strengths	Weaknesses
Excellence	Strong marketing & human resource benefits; Universally recognizable—mark of uncompromising standards & high achievement	Provides little practical guidance to practitioners; Measurement difficulties; Attributes of excellence may change dramatically and rapidly; Sufficient number of customers must be willing to pay for excellence
Value	Concept of value incorporates multiple attributes; Focuses attention on a firm's internal efficiency & external effectiveness; Allows for comparisons across disparate objects & experiences	Difficulty extracting individual components of value judgment; Questionable inclusiveness; Quality & value are different constructs
Conformance to Specifications	Facilitates precise measurement; Leads to increased efficiency; Necessary for global strategy; Should force disaggregation of consumer needs; Most parsimonious & appropriate definition for some customers	Consumers do not know or care about internal specifications; Inappropriate for services; Potentially reduces organizational specifications; may quickly become obsolete in rapidly changing markets; Internally focused
Meeting and/or Exceeding Expectations	Evaluates from customer's perspective; Applicable across industries; Responsive to market changes; All-encompassing definition	Most complex definition; Difficult to measure; Customers may not know expectations; Idiosyncratic reactions; Pre-purchase attitudes affect subsequent judgments; Short-term & long-term evaluations may differ; Confusion between customer service & customer satisfaction

[a] Source: Reeves & Bednar (1994), p. 437. Reprinted with permission.

- Proactive communications;
- Honesty and openness;
- Systems reliability;
- Swift reparation; and
- Little extras. (p. 2)

Service quality begins with the staff's recognition that there is a new way to do business. Front-line employees not committed to service quality can blur the service focus that managers want to convey.

Zeithaml, Parasuraman, and Berry (1990, p. 19) define service quality as "the extent of discrepancy between customers' expectations or desires and their perceptions." Drawing upon their previous work, they list 10 dimensions of service quality:

- *Tangibles.* Appearance of physical facilities, equipment, personnel, and communication materials;
- *Reliability.* Ability to perform the promised service dependably and accurately;
- *Responsiveness.* Willingness to help customers and provide prompt service;
- *Courtesy.* Politeness, respect, and friendliness of contact personnel;
- *Empathy.* Caring and individualized attention that the firm provides its customers;
- *Competence.* Required skills and knowledge to perform the service, believability, and honesty of the service provider;
- *Security.* Freedom from danger, risk, or doubt;
- *Access.* Approachability and ease of contact;
- *Communication.* Keeping the customers informed in language they can understand and listening to them; and
- *Understanding the customer.* Making the effort to know customers and their needs. (pp. 22–23, 26)

The authors then developed five broader dimensions of service quality: tangibles, reliability, and responsiveness (the same as those listed above). To these, they added *assurance,* which encompassed communication, credibility, security, competence, and courtesy; and *empathy,* which included access and understanding the customer (Zeithaml, Parasuraman, & Berry, 1990, pp. 25–26). They maintained that word of mouth, personal needs, past experiences, and external communications shape service expectations (p. 23). They also indicated where gaps between expectations and perceptions might exist, and offered suggestions for reducing the gaps.

Firms wishing to increase their "market orientation" must view customers as persons "with legitimate needs" and empower employees to "build a shared perspective with customers" (McQuarrie, 1993, p. 8). In its "Annual Meeting Report," the International Business Machines Corporation (1994) (IBM) discusses the corporation's need "to get closer to our customers" if "we...(are) going to grow" (p. 3). Customer needs must be met if the corporation is to improve market share, the report goes on to observe; product reliability is only one component of quality. Customers recognize poor service; consequently, superior service must be delivered in processes as well as products. Moreover, as the literature suggests, quality service is an attitude that requires: (a) employees to be dissatisfied with the status quo, (b) a continuous striving for perfection, and (c) a commitment to the importance of the customer. The rewards of quality service are high morale among employees and loyalty among clients; it is a win–win game, but requires a long-term commitment and teamwork. As F. J. McDonald, a president of General Motors, observed, "The environment has to be one that is error-friendly. Quality is error driven. It depends on each individual's ability to recognize error trends and to make corrections quickly" (Humphries & Naisawald, 1991, p. 265).

Blueprints for Service Quality—The Federal Express Approach (1991) is an important work on service quality, and it documents the attributes that make Federal Express an outstanding service organization. The company has consistent, clearly stated service goals and measures for service failures, and it views employee satisfaction as the source of customer satisfaction and financial success. The company recognizes that its staff is its single most valuable resource. All departments work toward the common goals of good response time and courteous service at the promised cost, which result in fulfillment of its service commitment and, consequently, customer satisfaction. Customer surveys are used to identify the problems most likely to cause dissatisfaction, and problems are ranked according to how angry they make customers. The company determines how often each problem occurs, factors this into its rankings, and arrives at the total number of daily "failures," which it works to reduce (Galagan, 1991, p. 29). In effect, Federal Express said, "Of all the data that we collect, we consider those relating to service failures to assume high priority." The company links employees' knowledge of their jobs to their salary level and assesses their job knowledge every six months. In addition to an audit procedure, there is an active program for training employees upon which "the company spends 3% of its total expenses, or about $225 millions a year" (p. 29). (As an aside, Zemke with Schaaf (1989) offered suggestions around which a training program might be built.)

Higher Education

As Rush (1992, p. 39) noted, "The challenge (for higher education) is not how to merely survive with fewer funds in the future but how to *thrive* with less money" (ital added). As colleges and universities increasingly focus on applying the best business practices in order "to deliver value for money"—becoming more productive, setting meaningful goals, and becoming accountable for achieving them (Massy, 1994, p. 29; see also Hague, 1991, pp. 12-13) [4,5]—they will begin to define quality more as meeting or exceeding the needs and expectations of *customers*. Educational institutions "are in a competitive battle for students, and students are (both products and) customers" (Sines & Duckworth, 1994, p. 2). Institutions experiencing problems in attracting and retaining students have begun to realize that "students are increasingly seeking out those institutions offering them the treatment they believe they deserve as paying customers" (p. 2).[6]

Students do not comprise the only category of customers of institutions of higher learning; parents, government officials, and groups internal to the institution (administrators, faculty, and staff) are also customers. Adopting a customer focus moves attention from a comparison of data or statistics among comparable institutions to an examination of one institution and its constituent groups. Moreover, the adage that the "customer is always right" does not apply to service quality. Service quality does not deal with issues of right or wrong.

Institutions of higher education need to identify service and system failures (i.e., areas needing improvement), as well as reasons for dissatisfaction, and to take corrective action as necessary. They need to adopt an "employee-focused approach: quality circles, quality teams, or employee involvement" (Sines & Duckworth, 1994, p. 7). Clearly, the 10 stages of service quality developed by Stafford (1994) apply to higher education.

By embracing service quality, colleges and universities can develop new types of measures—*outcome* measures— that enable them to assess areas such as:

---

[4] "To regain the public trust, colleges and universities must redefine their goals to emphasize more than prestige and its main driver, faculty research. The new goals must focus on the needs of the undergraduate and professional clients whose education represents the primary mission for most institutions and the objectives of those who provide the funding for them. While research should continue to be important, accountability requires that institutions demonstrate a reasonable balance between the resources dedicated to research and those used for education." (Massy, 1994, p. 36)

[5] "Colleges and universities should reflect on their mission and its implications for the education-research balance, redefine undergraduate education in terms of client need and value for money, redouble their efforts to maintain financial discipline, and develop appropriate performance measures. The objective should be significant quality improvements and cost reductions in areas not essential to the central academic mission—in other words, institutional restructuring." (Massy, 1994, p. 38)

[6] "What determines a quality education is more than just what takes place in the classroom. It should be considered as everything that takes place on the campus, and everything the student does to get and stay in the classroom has to be considered as part of a quality education." (Sines & Duckworth, 1994, p. 3)

$$\frac{\text{Number of students who transfer}}{\text{Number of students at the institution}} = \underline{\quad}\%$$

$$\frac{\begin{array}{c}\text{Number of students getting accepted}\\\text{by the graduate school/program of choice}\end{array}}{\begin{array}{c}\text{Number of graduating students applying}\\\text{to graduate schools/programs}\end{array}} = \underline{\quad}\%$$

$$\frac{\begin{array}{c}\text{Number of students attending graduate}\\\text{school at the college/university}\end{array}}{\begin{array}{c}\text{Number of graduating students interested}\\\text{in a graduate degree offered by the}\\\text{college/university}\end{array}} = \underline{\quad}\%$$

It is also possible to produce measures that address only master's or doctoral programs.

Library and Information Science

Institutions of higher education and different constituent groups support libraries on the premise that they play a role in enabling the institution to meet its mission by providing information; learning experiences; and high quality collections, services, and programs at a reasonable cost. Since the 1980s, librarians and others have expressed concern about the failure of library funding to keep pace with inflation, and they have lamented dramatic cuts in collections and services. At the same time, technology has presented new challenges and opportunities.

"As academic libraries continue to evolve as service organizations" (Millson-Martula & Menon, 1995, p. 33), they should improve the ability of constituent groups to use services, products, and collections effectively and efficiently, and to expect (and receive) a certain level of service quality. A library, like any organization, must determine, monitor, and improve its service-oriented image,[7] be accountable, and be responsive to the information

---

[7] That image, in the mind of a customer, in part, might be formed at "a moment of truth... that precise instant when the customer comes into contact with any aspect of your business and, on the basis of that contact, forms an opinion about the quality of your service and potentially the quality of your product" (Brown, 1994, p. 213). Brown (p. 214) asks an important question: "What happens if reference librarians don't manage moments of truth well?" To this, we add "What if all library staff do not handle these moments well?" After all, technical service and other staff contribute to the ability of the library to cope with moments of truth.

needs of its customers. Are the library's image and the service it provides reflective of quality conscientiousness, innovation, and customer orientation (Lytle, 1993, p. 145)? An unsatisfactory image may encourage unreasonable expectations in customers and cause them to turn to another library or service provider. In effect, "Quality must become a valued characteristic of every customer interaction" (Humphries & Naisawald, 1991, p. 265).

A problem unique to some libraries is their open-door policy of serving more than their immediate constituent groups: They try to offer something to everyone. In the electronic information age, they may attempt more than they can effectively accomplish and as a result, they do poorly. In this regard, the number of transactions completed is an unreliable indicator of service quality. Service quality involves the strategic deployment of resources to narrow the gap between what the organization and customers expect and the services provided (see Table 3.2).

Bicknell (1994, p. 80) pointed out that because "each library has its own unique clientele, building, and philosophy of service... each library's program of quality reference service will have its own unique aspects." Marketing and other literatures make a stronger point: firms continuously strive to improve themselves while seeking market advantage. Libraries may not be in competition with other libraries, but they do compete with other service providers, especially in the realm of electronic information provision.

As Millson-Martula and Menon (1995) commented:

> The continued success of a service organization such as an academic library depends upon the organization's ability to adjust its products and services to correspond to user needs. Academic librarians need to realize that student and faculty needs do change. The change may not be radical or monumental. However, even in the case of subtle or evolutionary change, it remains incumbent for librarians to: (1) be aware that needs are changing; (2) understand the nature of the changes; and (3) realign or reconfigure services to ensure that they remain relevant to the recently developed needs. (p. 34)

To accomplish far-reaching change, the organization must be supportive; as Shaughnessy (1987) explained, "the commitment to [change and] quality must pervade the organization:"

> Building a culture for quality involves establishing specific quality standards, recruiting staff who have the capacity to meet those standards, training them to meet the standards, evaluating them accordingly, and rewarding them when they are successful. There is, therefore, a quality loop, and the loop must be closed. (p. 9)

As Edwards and Browne (1995) noted, "There are many reasons why users might perceive a service quality gap in an organization like a library [see Figure 3.1]. For example:

- Clients' expectations for the service and management's perceptions of these expectations may not match;
- Managers may not be able to translate clients' expectations effectively into services which meet users' expectations;
- The service which is delivered may not be consistent with service specifications;
- The service which is actually delivered and the information which is provided to the client about this service may not be congruent...; and
- The experience of the client and the providers' perceptions of these experiences may differ.[8] (p. 164)

"Although each of these reasons is crucial, the first reason for a gap is a fundamental point 'from which quality of service must be measured'" (Edwards & Browne, 1995, p. 164). Furthermore, "If there is a lack of congruence between users' expectations and providers' perceptions of these expectations, service quality will suffer regardless of how well services are planned, delivered, and marketed" (p. 164). "This potential mismatch" (p. 164) should be documented and addressed. St. Clair (1993) offers an excellent discussion on "nurturing" a climate of change in which management and staff work together (pp. 54–64) to reduce gaps and to involve users in the process (pp. 65–74).

Plum (1994) made an interesting distinction regarding types of knowledge. He said knowing something is knowledge; knowing how to find something is ritual knowledge. Library patrons hope to acquire knowledge, whereas library staff focus on ritual knowledge. Thus, it is important that service not focus on the ritual knowledge to the exclusion of knowledge itself. Clearly, libraries must understand and differentiate between customer *wants* and *needs,* while working to minimize any gap between the two. Contrary to some misperceptions, service quality does not mean merely giving customers what librarians think customers want; for example, providing students with term papers to copy. Such misperceptions distort the importance of service quality to library planning and evaluation. However, customers may have to be trained not to want things they do not need.

As part of a customer-service plan (St. Clair, 1993), librarians should develop and support customer-service training programs that deal with han-

---

[8] Zeithaml, Parasuraman, and Berry (1990, p. 40) collapse the same gaps into four groups. Millson-Martula and Menon (1995, pp. 40–41) speculate about the factors leading to each gap, and they offer remedies for gap reduction.

dling customers and address inadequacies in service-delivery systems (Arthur, 1994, p. 222).[9] It is important to address such points since "all contacts with an organization are a critical part of our perceptions and judgements about that organization" (Albrecht & Zemke, 1985, p. 8).

Humphries and Naisawald (1991) developed a quality assurance program for evaluating online services in a health sciences library. Hébert (1994) examined the quality of interlibrary loan services from the perspective of both the library and its customers by using an unobtrusive method of data collection and a modified version of the SERVQUAL instrument developed by Zeithaml, Parasuraman, & Berry (1990), which uses gap analysis to measure service quality. Adopting the Grönroos model of service quality (1984), Hébert divided quality into two service dimensions:

- **Technical quality:** An objective measure of *what* customers receive in their interactions with a service organization; and
- **Functional quality:** A subjective measure of *how* customers receive a service. (Hébert, 1994, p. 5)

Functional quality indicates that customers are "influenced by the way in which technical quality is transferred to them functionally." "Technical and functional quality represent a bundle of services which together create the construct 'image' or attitude" (p. 5). It is possible "image may be a quality dimension capable of overriding substantial technical and functional service quality delivery" (p. 5).

Hébert (1994) found a mismatch between library measures of interlibrary loan performance, based on fill rate and turnaround time, and customer measures of quality, based on "disconfirmation theory" (p. 3).[10] As she explained, "When library and customer measures of quality are not congruent, the library may be meeting its internal standards of performance but may not be performing well in the eyes of its customers" (p. 20). Clearly, the library must improve both technical and functional quality.

Edwards and Browne (1995, p. 165) studied "the question of whether there are differences in the expectations which academics hold of information services provided by academic libraries, and librarians' perceptions of

---

[9] St. Clair (1993, p. 123) noted, "One of the major problems in any service operation is dealing with telephone queries, yet most information service managers do not concern themselves with the rudiments of telephone procedures in their organizations." He then offers 11 excellent suggestions for improving telephone service.

[10] Fill rate measures and "other current measures… evaluate performance only from the organizational perspective, equating quality to compliance with objective standards." Moreover, "the fill rate measures only the proportion of actual requests that are met, not the extent to which customer needs are met" (Hébert, 1994, p.4).

these expectations." They found that both groups:

> Have similar expectations but there are differences in the emphasis each...
> places on aspects of service. Librarians, for example, underestimate the impor-
> tance to academics of the responsiveness of a service and overestimated the
> importance of the characteristics of the staff who provide the service.(p. 163)[11]

Their findings are tentative and reflect a small sample of two constituent groups, librarians and faculty, in Australia. There may be substantial differences among other groups, countries, and types of institutions, ranging from community colleges to institutions offering doctoral programs.

Danuta A. Nitecki, in a presentation before the Association of College and Research Libraries (ACRL) conference in Pittsburgh, Pennsylvania, on March 30, 1995, reported selected findings from her then in-progress dissertation that used the SERVQUAL instrument to compare service quality among interlibrary loan, reserve, and reference at one academic library. She compared her findings to those of Zeithaml, Parasuraman, and Berry (1990), who studied other service industries. During the question and answer period, Nitecki mentioned the libraries at Texas A&M University, the University of Wisconsin–Madison, and the University of Arizona are surveying their customers using the SERVQUAL instrument.

White and Abels (1995) identified and assessed criticisms of the SERVQUAL scale. They considered the instrument to be "flexible" and adaptable to special libraries (p. 41). They suggested SERVPERF, an instrument developed in 1992 (Cronin & Taylor, 1992; 1994), has the same attributes and provides "a performance-based measure of service quality" (White & Abels, 1995, p. 40). They noted:

> SERVPERF is less complex, shorter, easier to administer, and better in pre-
> dicting overall variance. SERVQUAL, on the other hand, is attractive because
> it is more comprehensive. It provides better diagnostic information, and, if
> desired, the performance data alone can be used to explain overall variance.
> Because it has been used more widely, SERVQUAL also allows for greater

---

[11] According to Edwards and Browne (1995, pp. 180–181), "The librarians' responses suggested that they overestimate the importance of the *assurance* factor, that is, the extent to which they as service providers are knowledgeable and courteous, and engender a feeling of trust and confidence in the service being provided. The users appear to be more focused on what they came to the library for, rather than on the characteristics of the people who provide it. They are not quite so concerned with the competence of the librarians or the politeness, friendliness, or the impression of trustworthiness they give. Clearly, it is important to provide a degree of civility and competence in a service, but information services managers need to recognize this as a means and not an end in itself....The tangibles of a service, such as the physical surroundings and appearance of staff are not, in the minds of users, central to the provision of an excellent service."

comparability with other service organizations.

Both instruments are oriented to overall performance quality, not to the quality of specific services; they are generic instruments. Both draw on the same items, whose wording would have to be modified slightly to fit library settings.

The dimensions covered by both are the same and seem appropriate for libraries. (p. 41)

As is evident, research in special and academic libraries in the United States, and Australian and Canadian libraries, is exploring the dimensions that characterize "the range of values (that certain groups of) library clients attach to information services" (p. 42).

The research of Hébert, Edwards and Browne, Nitecki, and White and Abels is an important first step for measuring service quality provided by libraries. They are developing data collection instruments to measure the gap between expectations and services actually provided. The next step should be to join these different research efforts to produce a common standardized test, certified for its reliability and validity, which applies to libraries.[12]

Hernon and Altman (1995) took an entirely different approach to studying service quality. They believe that it is essential to develop a framework for viewing service quality based on case study research (see Table 3.3) and then to select components from the framework for examination. In other words, the first step is to understand that service quality refers to the *product* (information content), *service environment,* and *service delivery.* They suggested two important input measures that affect service delivery: staff morale and workload. Obviously, the quality of service delivery declines as morale decreases and workload increases.

Because the libraries of today and tomorrow are less place-bound, service quality must be applied to different contexts. There is still a physical library building and collections, but access and services transcend the setting. Through OhioLINK, a statewide network in Ohio, people throughout the state can use online catalogs of various libraries to search for needed titles (see Hirshon, 1995). The network accepts user requests and spreads the responsibility of supplying the titles among participating libraries. Each day, the libraries gather the requested titles and ship them, via a courier service, to the library served by the user. Receipt of requested titles within 48 hours of making a request has raised customer expectations and vastly improved service delivery and response time.

Kaske (1994) argued performance measures, and by extension outcome

---

[12] A listserv, "Measurement of Product and Service Quality," provides a forum for discussion of the measurement of product and service quality. The forum also intends to make available to organizations different instruments for the measurement of product and service quality. To subscribe to the listserv, send an e-mail message to: TQM@cua.cameron.edu, and put as the subject of the message: TQM: subscribe.

Table 3.3.   Service Quality: A Framework [a]

Product: Information Content

1. Accessibility   2. Accuracy   3. Currentness or Timeliness   4. Degree of Comprehensiveness
5. Packaging: Aesthetics   6. Relevance (see Wilson, 1995)   7. Understandability

Service Environment

1. Physical Surroundings
    a. Ambient Conditions
    b. Signage
    c. Spatial Layout
2. Convenience
    a. Hours
    b. Location
3. Choices
    a. Source of service (which library; CARL UnCover versus paper copy versus CD-ROM; etc.)
    b. Means of Delivery (fax, etc.)
4. Availability—Accessibility
    a. Information
    b. Facilities & Equipment
        1. In operating condition
    c. Staff, including service time—amount of time waiting in lines
5. Service Reputation
6. Complaint Procedures (see St. Clair, 1993, pp. 133–135)
    a. Ease of Complaining
7. Redress for Receiving Poor Service

Service Delivery: Staff

A. Public Service Staff
    1. Knowledge
        a. Subject
        b. Issues, (e.g., intellectual property rights)
    2. Accuracy
    3. Behavior
        a. Approachable
        b. Courteous
        c. Empathetic
        d. Friendly
    4. Communication Skills
        a. Ability to Determine What Customer Wants
    5. Speed of Delivery
    6. *Sufficient* Amount of Assistance Provided, including the Amount of Time Needed to
        Respond to Request
B. Technical Service Staff
    1. Knowledge of User Needs
    2. Knowledge of Information-Seeking Behavior
    3. Accuracy and Speed of Delivery (e.g., in Ordering & Processing)

[a] Adapted from Hernon & Altman (1995, p. 33) with permission.

measures and service models, must take into account the growth of electronic information and the emergence of national or global information infrastructures. There are increased opportunities for patrons to search library systems online and request items directly from another library or provider: "Patrons are no longer limited to one library; in fact, they (may) use many libraries in their search for information items" (p. 317). As a result, "Today's library clearly does not have walls" (p. 317). Chapter 4 reviews the framework depicted in Table 3.3 and suggests which elements apply to information superhighways.

Sirkin (1993, p. 80) maintained, "A strategic focus on customer service and satisfaction is an effective tool to help librarians accomplish their mission," and offered pertinent suggestions and examples (pp. 82–83).

Because service quality and customer satisfaction are intended to produce repeat business, an important measure of satisfaction is willingness to return to the same library and certain staff members again. Such willingness can be quantified and converted to a general outcome measure by dividing willingness to use the library or request assistance from the same staff member by number of customers (e.g., student) served. This measure serves as a reminder that service quality and satisfaction are linked; however, quality involves more than satisfaction. Service quality deals at the macro level and satisfaction covers the micro level.

Dewdney and Ross (1994), who reported on student experiences in using academic and public libraries, concluded "Both willingness to return and overall satisfaction were significantly related to the librarian's behavior and the quality of the answer" (p. 217). They explored "most helpful" and "least helpful" features of services received as ranked by the students. This ranking showed the relative importance of reference staff smiling and displaying welcoming body language, of eye contact, of the ability and willingness to pursue a reference interview beyond the initial question asked, of use of a follow-up question to invite users to return, of moving away from the desk, of including users in the search process, and of unmonitored referrals in which staff members give patrons a call number or refer them "to a source in the library thought to contain the answer but...(do) not follow up or check to make sure that the source is not only found but actually answers the question" (p. 227). Dewdney and Ross emphasized the importance of making an effort to assure the success of the information seeker.

They found that approximately "one-third of the time...users decided to cut their losses and start the search anew with another librarian or in another library" (p. 228). "This finding," they noted, raises "serious questions about the (potential) waste of human resources that such duplication entails" (p. 228).

Dewdney and Ross found certain variables (overall satisfaction, willingness to return, friendliness, understanding, and helpfulness of the answer) were significantly correlated "with the strongest relationship found between the user's overall satisfaction and the helpfulness of the answer $(r=.81, p<.05)$." Furthermore, "consistent with Durrance's [1989] findings, the relationship between overall satisfaction and the friendliness of the staff member was strongly correlated $(r=.71, p<.05)$" (p. 223).[13]

Their study:

> Suggests that the 55 percent rule—on average, reference staff provide correct answers to only 55 percent of the questions they get—may still be alive and well, whether we measure the outcome of the reference transaction in terms of accuracy, helpfulness of the answer, overall satisfaction, or willingness to return to the same staff member. (p. 228)

As a partial remedy for improving reference service, they encouraged staff to take programs in communication training (p. 228) and suggested an example of such a program as well as some applications (note 17, p. 230).

The British Library's *Strategic Objectives for the Year 2000* (The British Library, 1993) is an important reminder that service quality appeals to more than librarians in the United States and researchers in the countries already noted. The Library promises "high quality service within available budgets" (p. 15). In fact, it has developed "service delivery targets for the year 2000" (pp. 37–38). As well, the British Library has a measurable "Code of Service" for each division (The British Library, 1994).

SOFTWARE

Surveytools Corporation (276 Oakland St., Wellesley, MA 02181; telephone: 671-431-1255) is developing *The Beneserve™ Customer Satisfaction System,* which will consist of two manuals and a software program.[14] Its purpose is to provide businesses with a framework and procedure for understanding and measuring both customer satisfaction and aspects of service quality. Businesses are instructed to "think like a

---

[13] Dewdney and Ross (1994, p. 222) defined *friendliness* as, "To what extent would you say the librarian was friendly or pleasant?;" *understanding* as, "By the end of your conversation, how well did the librarian seem to understand what you really wanted?;" *helpfulness of the answer* as, "How helpful was the answer given, in terms of your own needs?;" and *overall satisfaction* as, "How satisfactory was your experience, as a whole?"

[14] Both the questionnaire and software could easily be adapted to meet the needs of libraries and other organizations.

customer" and to measure "how well you're doing, just like the pulse rate and temperature of a patient tells the doctor how the patient is doing" (Whitman, 1995, p. 9).

The Beneserve Manual contains an interesting and relevant exercise (Whitman, 1995, pp. 15–16) in which management, employees, and a few customers are asked to "compile a list of [service] dimensions that define...(the) business (and)...describe (the) service." Examples of most valuable dimensions might include:

- Ability to understand your needs;
- Accuracy;
- Ambiance/atmosphere;
- Availability of personnel;
- Commitment to service;
- Customer education programs;
- Guarantee of satisfaction;
- Follow-up after sale;
- Level of attention;
- Level of knowledge;
- Overall value for the price;
- Physical facility;
- Service manner; and
- Telephone manner.

These dimensions, which apply to libraries, inform customers what to expect from the service provided and ensure the business views service expectations from a customer perspective. The purpose is to identify the essential dimensions and to measure the extent to which customers' expectations are met. Such an approach reinforces that the primary intent of service quality is gap reduction: reduction in the differences between expectations and services provided (see Figure 3.1 and Table 3.2).

Surveytools Corp. also produces *Benevox*™, a software program for "creating and measuring public satisfaction in civic educational facilities" (such as libraries). The program contains a flexible instrument for documenting customer satisfaction with libraries and other organizations. Nonetheless, the software and companion instrument ask three questions relevant for gauging service failures (i.e., areas needing improvement): "What are the *best* things about us?," "What are the *worst* things about us?," and "If we could do *one thing* to improve, what would it be?" Using the inexpensive software, it is possible to compile a list of responses to the three open-ended questions, and to compare responses over time (producing report cards) to monitor changes in perceptions.

APPLICATION OF THE LITERATURE TO
THE EVALUATION OF LIBRARIES FROM
A CUSTOMER FOCUS

As shown in *Measure Up!* (Lynch & Cross, 1991), quality is distinct from customer satisfaction, and both must be viewed within the framework of the organization's mission and vision. The mission answers "'Why does this entity exist?'(a variant might be, 'What difference does it make that this institution exists?')" (Bergquist, 1995, p. 253). Ayers (1995, p. 20) defined vision as "the concept or picture of what your organization can or should be; it requires that you fulfill the unmet needs of your customers;" vision focuses on the customer, more than on the institution.[15]

Viewing quality within the context of gap reduction enables higher education administrators to recognize:

> Quality exists when adequate and appropriate resources are being directed successfully toward the accomplishment of mission-related institutional outcomes and when programs make a significant and positive mission-related difference in the lives of people affiliated with the college or university and are created, conducted, and modified in a manner that is consistent with the mission and values of the institution. (Bergquist, 1995, p. 10)

Table 3.4 is an example of a college mission statement; its corresponding vision statement is, "Simmons College educates its diverse students for professional, personal, and community achievement in the global societies of the twenty-first century" ("Simmons College Vision Statement," 1994, unpaged). Institutions may choose to develop separate vision statements for undergraduate and graduate programs.

The institution's library should adopt mission and vision statements showing the library's role and responsibility in meeting the mission and vision of the institution (see St Clair, 1993, pp. 21–26). Cipolla (1987), Hardesty, Hastreiter, and Henderson (1985), and McClure et al. (1987), offered examples of library mission statements; Siggins and Sullivan (1993) reprinted vision statements for some libraries that belong to the Association of Research Libraries (ARL).

Clack (1995) reproduced the mission statement for Harvard College Library and offered a "working document on values" (pp. 151–152). The first value, "access/service and collections/scholarship," affirms the library's responsibility to its user community, while Appendix A of the article speculates about the "Library, Ten Years Hence" (pp. 150–151).

---

[15] Meyer (1995, p. 336) argued, "The issue is to figure out what our...[institutions] offer and use that knowledge to determine a vision for the library."

Table 3.4. Simmons College Statement of Mission [a]

Simmons College was founded in 1899 as a college designed to educate women for fulfilling careers and useful, independent lives. Today, Simmons continues its tradition of excellence through a focus on liberal arts and sciences and professional education in our undergraduate programs for women and our graduate programs for women and men. Faculty and staff in all areas of the College, building upon their own scholarly accomplishment and continuing professional development, strive to provide a student-centered environment and a curriculum that is comprehensive, integrated and constantly renewed.

All Simmons programs reflect a belief in the following premises:
- A Simmons education empowers students and develops their capacity for critical thinking, the bold pursuit of new ideas, cooperation, and leadership.
- The world's many cultures, nationalities, and ethnicities challenge Simmons to shape an educational community reflective of and strengthened by individual differences.
- Beyond the campus, Boston's dynamic and diverse urban community is a Simmons classroom where all have the opportunity to be educated and enriched.
- Education at Simmons instills in students a passion for lifelong learning, a commitment to involved citizenship, sensitivity to the world community, and the self-confidence to speak with an individual voice.

Recognizing the challenges that will face Simmons graduates in the 21st century, the faculty, staff, administration, alumni, and Corporation of Simmons College are committed to this mission, and we hold ourselves accountable for its fulfillment.

[a] "Simmons College Statement of Mission" (1994). Reprinted with permission.

St. Clair (1993) noted:

Customer (user) needs drive the information services unit [i.e., library] and the mission statement of the unit, which states the reason for the unit's existence, the scope of the unit's activities, direction of the unit, and serves as a basis for the unit's objectives and plans, leads to the support of the mission of the parent organization, the enterprise, or the community. (p. 23)

A vision statement might focus on the types of collections and services necessary to meet the institution's vision of being responsive to its customers or constituencies. Of course, national and global information infrastructures and the Internet, as well as the concept of information literacy, may be important components for meeting a long-term vision.

Academic libraries have many audiences for whom they must demonstrate accountability, including regional accrediting associations, the federal government and perhaps state government, and the institution itself. As managers, librarians must justify expenditures, decisions, and strategic directions. To this end, they might collect input and output data, and performance measures, or in some way demonstrate the extent to which programs, services, and operations are effective and efficient (see Chapter 2).

Van House and Childers (1993, p. 1) asked questions to help place the concept of effectiveness within a framework:

- What is an effective organization?
- How do we know effectiveness when we see it?
- What makes an organization effective?

Service quality is not synonymous with effectiveness, but it does provide insights from the customers' perspective—those constituent groups that benefit directly from library's collections, programs, and services.

LOOKING AHEAD

This book views service quality as a means of reducing the gap between customer expectations and needs (see Figure 3.1), and as a synonym for excellence (see Table 3.2). Organizations address quality within the context of their mission and service visions. As *Blueprints for Service Quality—The Federal Express Approach* (1991) emphasizes, the key to customer satisfaction and service quality is a satisfied workforce, meaning that managers must first devote attention to internal customers (employees) before they can expect external customers to be satisfied: "Libraries accomplish their goals through their employees. If the employees don't perform, the library does not perform" (Walters, 1994, p. 25). An investment in staff training and workplace education is an absolute necessity if service quality is to be realized (see Donnelly, 1992; Galagan, 1991).

"Service-oriented organizations concentrate on creating an *environment* in which customers are valued and providing good service is the norm" (Disend, 1991, p. 120). Customers should know what to expect of the organization; customer service standards assist in this attempt and reflect a determined effort to provide exceptional service. It is possible for a library to be guided by different service standards; however, customer groups must be aware of the standards and not regard them as contradictory or confusing. Furthermore, both librarians and their customers "need to recognize what we (librarians) do and do...well, rather than trying to expand our professional turf by convincing the world that any information need is best dealt with by a [library and a] librarian" (Westbrook, 1994, p. 345). Service standards must be measurable, using either quantitative or qualitative methods of data collection, or both.

Service quality deals with market segments (separating customers into different constituent groups and aggregating data from each group into a composite picture of the whole) (see Davidow & Uttal, 1989), and *outcome* measures reflect customer views on service quality. Service quality encourages evaluators to move away from input and performance measures. What matters more than an organization's customers? Obviously libraries must not rule out other ways of examining issues, but the question remains an important reminder that libraries, while adopting more of a customer focus, should not necessarily regard all customers' viewpoints as equal or requiring action (Tjosvold, 1993). Furthermore, service quality is subjective and individualistic. Nonetheless, "managers and researchers must account for the trade-offs inherent in the different quality definitions used by relevant constituencies" (Reeves & Bednar, 1994, p. 440).

As Berry, Bennett, and Brown (1989, p. 8) explained, "Most customers want good service and some of them will go elsewhere if they don't get it. That, however, is where it stops being simple." There are many obstacles to good service: An extensive number of customers to reach, numerous staff to train on a recurring basis, and a high number of daily transactions are everyday situations ripe with the potential for something to go amiss. Such complexities make service quality difficult to reach, but libraries cannot afford to postpone the difficult trip.

Sines and Duckworth (1994) noted:

> Technical Assistance programs (TARP), a customer service research and consulting firm headquartered in Washington, D.C., has published some interesting facts concerning customer satisfaction (which have implications for service quality in libraries):
>
> ➤ The average business will not hear from 96% of unhappy customers.
> ➤ For every person complaining, 26 will not complain.
> ➤ 13% of those having a problem with the organization will relate that experience to 20 or more people.
>
> When considering the cost to the organization for poor customer service, it is imperative that a program be instituted immediately. (pp. 7–8)

As this chapter suggests, libraries can begin to adopt a customer focus by reviewing their mission statement, developing a vision statement, and implementing a customer-service philosophy. They can then decide where to concentrate their evaluation efforts to achieve customer-service excellence (see Paul, 1990).

The University Libraries at Wright State University have pledged their "commitment to excellence." Table 3.5 reproduces the commitment and pledge. A number of the points, such as those related to "Information Delivery Services," are measurable within a specified time frame. The librarians have identified those points which they consider most important in meeting the needs of their customers. These points apply to both public and technical service staff, thereby casting the library as a system with each department contributing toward the common good—making the pledge and commitment a reality.

Table 3.5. Wright State University Libraries'
Pledge and Commitment to Excellence [a]

The staff of the University Libraries firmly commit to provide excellent customer service....You will find our general statement of commitment and specific standards of excellence for each service area. We continually evaluate and update these standards. We value your opinions. Please give us your comments and suggestions, and we will respond.

Sincerely,
Arnold Hirshon
University Librarian

Commitment to Excellence:

- We will provide courteous, prompt, and accurate service to every customer.
- We will carefully listen and respond to your needs.
- We will provide resources to meet your research needs.
- We will offer opportunities for instruction about our resources and services.
- We will provide an environment conducive to study and research.
- We will not give you the runaround. We will provide the assistance you need, or we will put you in contact with someone who can.

We pledge to:

General Services

- Acknowledge you immediately at any service desk and serve you within 3 minutes or call additional staff
- Call you back if we need to ask you to hold on the phone for more than 3 minutes
- Report photocopier problems to the University Printing Services immediately
- Respond personally to your signed suggestions within 5 working days
- Make the names and phone numbers of supervisors available at all service points
- Provide users with the tools and training to enable access to the University Libraries' collections and to resources available nationally
- Publicize changes in our services and provide opportunities for training for new services
- Maintain designated quiet study areas
- Provide a clean and comfortable study environment

Collections and Electronic Information Services

- Ensure that our collections support the instructional and research mission of Wright State University
- Ensure the high reliability of the LIBNET system including workstations capable of printing and/or downloading
- Catalog materials accurately and promptly
- Make new books available within 4 weeks of receipt and provide rush delivery when necessary
- Meet your research needs when materials are at the bindery by locating acceptable substitutes immediately or providing copies within 48 hours
- Respond to faculty book orders within 5 working days
- Meet each faculty representative or department chair at least once each quarter to review academic needs

Reference and Research Services

- Provide professional reference service to facilitate your successful use of library services, resources, and collections
- Offer scheduled appointments for extended reference consultations
- Complete database search requests within 2 working days
- Respond to online reference inquiries within 1 working day
- Assist faculty by developing presentations tailored to the needs of a class
- Assist faculty by providing reference support for specific assignments

Information Delivery Services

- Check out and check in all books and materials accurately and efficiently
- Fill OhioLINK requests within 2–3 days [b]
- Place your interlibrary loan requests within 2 days
- Shelve current periodicals within 24 hours of receipt
- Re-shelve books and bound periodicals within 24 hours of use and regularly maintain shelving order
- Re-shelve current periodicals within 1 hour of use
- Complete search requests within 24 hours

Special Collections Services

- Conduct an initial interview with you to meet your research needs most efficiently
- Locate materials housed on site within 5 minutes
- Complete photocopies of special collection materials within 48 hours
- Respond to telephone questions within 24 hours
- Submit requests for photographic copying to Media Services within 24 hours and send copies to you within 24 hours of completion

The final page of the customer service brochure states: "If you have any suggestions to improve this customer service statement or our operations, suggestion boxes are available on LIBNET and in the lobbies of both libraries. In addition, please contact [the names, phone numbers, and e-mail addresses of key departments and staff are given].

---

[a] Wright State University Libraries (1995).
[b] See Hirshon (1995).

This book, which takes a dramatic departure from other writings in library and information science, regards input, output, and performance measurement as outdated. We encourage their replacement with something more dynamic, such as *outcome* measures specifically related to customer-centered outcomes, and evaluation focused on areas needing improvement.[16] A key question becomes: "To what extent do/should/can libraries

---

[16] Hébert (1994, p. 10) found that the major areas in interlibrary loan needing improvement were unfilled requests, requests not located, requests refused, pickup problems, and requests not pursued. She concluded "that some libraries have created barriers to interlibrary loan, often unintentionally, through the behaviors of their staff" (p. 11). To improve service quality, libraries must reduce the barriers and make their staff more sensitive to the necessity of doing so.

Table 3.6. Comparison of Means of Data Collection: "Prose Versus Polls" [a]

Component	Open Letter	Telephone Survey	Written Survey	Focus Group
Opportunities for discovery	High	Low	Low	Moderate
Influence on respondent	None	Questionnaire	Questionnaire	Topic/questions
Moderator; Participants' Ability to probe	None	Limited	Limited	Substantial
Amount of information	Unlimited	Limited	Limited	Moderate
Sample size	Dependent on topic/ interest	Large	Large	Small
Sample representation	Self-selected	Random	Random	Screened
Costs	Publication cost; Data entry	List fees; Telephone charges; Interviewer salaries; Data entry	List fees; Print; Postage; Data entry	Pre-screen; Recruitment; Incentive; Travel; Moderator salary; Facilities; Discussion transcription

[a] Wylde (1994), p. 50. Table: "Prose Versus Polls," from "How to Read an Open Letter," September 1994 for use in *Service Quality in Academic Libraries.* Source: *American Demographics* magazine, © 1994. Reprinted with permission.

offer what customers value?"

There are different ways to collect data from internal and external customers, and to produce quality report cards at regular intervals (see Whitman, 1995, p. 105).[17] In Table 3.6, Wylde (1994, p. 50) compared "open-letter research with telephone surveys, written surveys, and

---

[17] "With people demanding better service" (Western, 1995, p. D2), more businesses employ mystery shoppers, or "customer service snoopers," to monitor employees' treatment of customers. These shoppers, unknown to the employees, visit the stores or make phone requests. In some instances, employees might know that, for instance, once a month they will serve a mystery shopper. Not knowing when the visit will be made or by whom, the presumption is that employees will regard everyone as a potential mystery shopper and offer quality service. In some instances, such experiences can be used as a tool for self-improvement or staff retention or relocation to other jobs.

focus groups."[18] She offered a strategy for gleaning "the rich diversity of information from...letters" and noted "any volunteered information will reveal the writer's attitudes, beliefs, behaviors, and actions" (p. 50). Nonetheless, such an approach will not reach the segment of dissatisfied customers who do not complain to the organization. Consequently, it is important to consider the use of both quantitative and qualitative methods of data collection that focus on service quality, not limited to those included in Table 3.6. Complementary methods include observation (see Berry, 1995; McQuarrie, 1993); completion of logs (see Brown, 1994); surveys (e.g., based on use of a SERVQUAL instrument) (see also St. Clair, 1993, pp. 75–91); formation of "quality circle groups" to identify and monitor problem areas and propose and monitor solutions (Brown, 1994, p. 217); and use of "quality improvement tools" (see Aluri, 1993). This book will suggest other ways to collect data relevant to planning and decision making.

Chapter 4 reviews and revises Table 3.3, thereby offering a more comprehensive representation of service quality. The chapter suggests some ways to gather data for the identification of areas needing improvement and elimination of problems (i.e., *service failures*), and it discusses the measurement of other aspects of service quality. Moreover, the chapter sets the stage for the development of: (a) outcome measures reflecting important service quality variables; and (b) a management information system for monitoring service quality throughout the organization. In summary, Chapters 4 through 7 provide a foundation from which library managers and staff can decide what to measure on a recurring basis.

The book is exploratory; it is intended to encourage a new direction in evaluation research applications, and to embrace both quantitative and qualitative measures. Nonetheless, there should be continued examination of the SERVQUAL instrument and eventually a union of that instrument with the procedures explored in this book (see Chapter 6). Together, they may provide an even richer understanding of service quality.[19] Case study research benefits from the use of triangulation or multi-methods of data collection.

---

[18] Library users, as well as library staff, should contribute open letters to "provide a picture of the problem areas" (Walters, 1994, p. 29). Feedback might also result from community forums, informal luncheon meetings (p. 50), and other techniques.

[19] Similarly, research should focus on sources of dissatisfaction and examine the findings within the context of service quality.

Chapter 4

Application of Service Quality to Academic Libraries

Library administration does not value service, but do the organizations in competition with libraries?

Students' time is not seen as important/valued.

Service quality means that librarians are here to give the best service to patrons without doing their research or getting burned out.

—Student survey comments

T he purpose of this chapter is to establish a common approach with which to measure and view service in academic libraries. The chapter specifically:

- Considers and modifies Table 3.3, the service quality framework;
- Identifies variables viewed as most important by academic librarians from an expansion of that table;
- Develops and applies two data collection instruments for gauging service quality and areas needing improvement;
- Identifies variables viewed as most important by customers of academic libraries; and
- Sets the stage for the discussion in subsequent chapters.

The exploratory research for this chapter was conducted in five phases. During phase one, we conducted focus group interviews at five academic libraries, ranging from baccalaureate-granting to doctoral-granting institutions (see Appendix C). The focus group interviews reviewed and more fully developed the components of Table 3.3, identified the most important variables in that table, gauged interest in service quality assessment, and pretested two data collection instruments (see Appendices A and B).

The second phase employed focus group interviews and in-person interviews to further refine the table and data collection instruments. The three focus group interviews, together with in-person interviews held at different institutions, represented a continuation of the first phase, but involved actual customers in the review process resulting in reassessment and modification of Tables 3.3 and 4.1 (see Table 4.2). In the third phase we conducted two focus group interviews—each at a different university library—in which participants were asked to identify the most important components of Table 4.2.

In phase four, the two data collection instruments were administered at three member libraries of the Association of Research Libraries (ARL). The surveys further reviewed Table 4.2, identified the variables that customers consider most important, and provided a foundation upon which other researchers can build.

The final phase centered around a presentation at the annual meeting of the AMIGOS Bibliographic Council, Inc., on May 3, 1995, in which we introduced our approach and some general findings to a diverse audience—comprised of more than just academic librarians—and sought feedback.

The research findings presented in this chapter result from the initiation of pilot projects designed to preview a way to measure service quality and produce data useful for benchmarking service quality locally and improving library planning and decision making.[1] The purpose is to provide data and insights for managing libraries as opposed to making comparisons to peer institutions. (What is new and different at the one institution over time?) The next chapters will demonstrate how librarians and researchers can refine our data collection instruments and procedures to identify areas needing improvement, to facilitate the gathering of trend data applicable to a local setting, or both.

PHASE ONE

Participants in each focus group interview reviewed Table 3.3 and assisted us with its modification. Table 4.1, which evolved over time, represents the col-

---

[1] For a discussion of benchmarking, see, for example, Chapter 6 and Balm (1992), Camp (1989), and Shaughnessy (1993).

lective views and perspectives of 37 librarians (see Appendix C). Although the clear intent was to illustrate the wide breadth of service quality, those interviewed were nevertheless frequently overwhelmed by the vast number of variables or components depicted. A typical response was, "I had no idea that service quality had so many aspects to it." Despite this feeling, participants still appreciated the opportunity to review the extensive listing of variables.

The librarians suspected a subset of variables reflected the most outstanding attributes of service quality. However, there were major differences both within and among libraries about which variables, in their opinion, were most important, indicating that librarians select variables to meet their own needs rather than to make comparisons across institutions. As a matter of fact, it might not always be productive to make comparisons among libraries within the same institution as it is not uncommon for branch and departmental libraries to have different jurisdictions, purposes, and clientele.

As review of Tables 3.3 and 4.1 illustrates, service quality is customer-focused, reflects customer expectations, and is a flexible concept that permits librarians to choose the aspects with which they want to deal. Furthermore, an analysis of service quality should provide data useful for local planning and decision making. Those interviewed realized individual libraries might add to or subtract from the components of Table 4.1, and select different key components from the table around which to conduct evaluation studies and explore outcome measures. After all, different customers have different expectations. Our purpose, however, was not to search for differences among customer groups. We leave this investigation to others.

The most important variables associated with electronic services, as identified by interviewees (regardless of their location), were accuracy ("resources: information content"); convenience and equipment ("the organization"); and technical expertise ("service delivery: staff"). However, the librarians at the final focus group site stressed that in dealing with, and in teaching students to use, electronic products and services, packaging, relevance, timeliness, degree of comprehensiveness, and appropriateness of fit were as important as accuracy. They emphasized the significance of appropriateness of fit when students encounter the World Wide Web and discover that what they initially thought might be good was, in fact, disappointing. Appropriateness of fit incorporates "content."

Focus group participants found it difficult to select the most important variables overall, but they suggested, as likely candidates, appropriateness of fit, accuracy, relevance, and currency of content (*resources*); choices and convenience under availability/accessibility (*the organization*); and ability to determine what the customer needs "or is willing to settle for" (*service delivery*). At one site, under "service delivery," "the librarians highlighted

Table 4.1. Service Quality: A Revised Framework

Resources: Information Content

1. Appropriateness of fit (match) between content and customer
2. Accuracy/trustworthiness
   - Degree of correctness (misinformation)
   - Inaccuracy: Subject to misconduct, e.g., fraud (disinformation)
3. Currentness or timeliness
4. Degree of comprehensiveness (e.g., thoroughness and extent to which an electronic product duplicates a print source)
5. Medium
6. Packaging: Aesthetics
7. Relevance (see Wilson, 1995)

The Organization: Its Service Environment and Resource Delivery

1. Availability/accessibility
   - Choices
     - Medium
     - Means of delivery (e.g., fax)
     - Source of service (e.g., a particular library or CARL Uncover)
   - Convenience
     - Assistance for electronic services (e.g., help screens, online tutorials, and publicized phone numbers for assistance)
     - Hours
     - Location (e.g., of library or collection)
     - Staffing (service time and availability)—queuing
   - Equipment—in operating condition
   - Information itself (ease of its use)
2. Responsiveness, including Complaint/Compliment Procedures
   - Ease of making complaint or compliment
   - Response for receiving *good* service
   - Response/redress for receiving *poor* service
3. Physical condition of materials in collection (e.g., brittle/materials or restricted use and photocopying)
4. Physical surroundings
   - Ambient conditions
   - Point of public service contact (e.g., branch libraries might have circulation, not reference, desks)
   - Signage
   - Spatial layout
5. Service costs
6. Service reputation (e.g., as service-oriented)

Service Delivery: Staff [a]

1. Ability to train/educate customers (e.g., in use of CD-ROM products)
2. Accuracy in answering questions
3. Behavior
   - Approachable
   - Appropriate body language and a smile

- Courteous
- Empathetic
- Friendly/pleasant
- Include user in search process (i.e., not ignoring his/her presence)
- Maintain eye contact
- Willingness to leave the desk

4. Communication skills
    - Ability to communicate with staff in other units of the library
    - Ability to determine what customer needs
    - Ability to negotiate library system and records (e.g., the library's and other libraries' catalogs, and MARC records) to assist customers
    - Conduct reference interview going beyond the initial question asked
    - Use follow-up question inviting user to return (willingness to return)

5. Knowledge
    - Issues (e.g., intellectual property rights)
    - Referral
    - Subject
    - Technical expertise (e.g., formats, accessing electronic information, and Internet access)

6. Speed of delivery (mechanical and human)

7. *Sufficient* amount of assistance provided, including the amount of time needed to respond to a request

Systems/Technical Service Staff

1. Ability to communicate with staff in other units of the library
2. Accuracy
3. Knowledge of (and ability to anticipate) user needs and information-seeking behavior
4. Knowledge of standards
5. Service orientation
6. Speed of delivery (e.g., in order & processing)
7. Technical knowledge of systems (e.g., technology-based)

---

[a] In some libraries, staff may perform both public and technical service functions.

---

behavior, communication skills, and knowledge." Librarians at two sites mentioned that, under behavior, willingness to return is a critical factor for measuring service quality.

In summary, the interviews conducted during the first phase indicate librarians could not necessarily agree on the applicability of a common set of variables within one library or library system and certainly not across institutions. They naturally focused on their local situations and selected variables accordingly. Variables such as accuracy and willingness to return are important but, of course, neither adequately defines service quality overall. Service quality is multi-dimensional, and librarians liked the opportunity to select those variables most meaningful to their particular managerial needs.

Service quality is definitely focused on the library as a system. An interdependency exists among library departments, and we were told that various staff members, in some instances, must learn to work together better. Unity and common vision, especially for the provision of electronic services, require a dedicated managerial team that encourages cooperation and innovation. At the same time, staff members may want to explore and improve their performances relative to variables such as behavior and communication skills while coping with customers unaware of the scope and breadth of library collections. One interviewee explained that the library is like a grocery store:

> We have so much to offer. However, if we do not have the product that customers want, we must direct them to another business. At the same time, we need to review our stock and see that we have a good selection of the products that our customers want and, at times, are willing to pay for. When we do not have what they want or they are unsure about what they want, we might persuade them that they need or should settle for a different product. However, this can be delicate; we need to do this in a way that makes our customers supportive, willing to return, and dependent on our products and services. Definitely, communications skills and behavior are critical components of service quality.

Phase two continues the process of identifying variables related to service quality.

PHASE TWO

We returned to three libraries that were involved in the first phase and asked focus group participants to review Table 4.1. They made further modifications (see Table 4.2) and commented on the two data collection instruments, *Service Quality for Library Users* and *Library Customer Survey*; Appendices A and B are the versions finally adopted.

We then conducted in-person interviews with customers at three different institutions to gather their perspectives on service quality. At one site, we interviewed students in a program of library and information science; the other two sites involved other customer groups.

Pretesting the First Questionnaire (Appendix A)

Students in a graduate program of library and information science participated in two focus group interviews geared to review Table 4.1 from the perspective of student customers knowledgeable about libraries. Based on their comments, the table was further refined; Table 4.2 is the replacement table.

Twenty students (7 doctoral and 13 master's) completed the survey. Seventeen (85%) used the college library's collections and services at least once a week and 7 (35%) used the library daily.

Of the 20, 16 (80%) had encountered areas needing improvement. All of the identified areas related to "the organization" or "service delivery: staff" (see Table 4.2). The most frequently mentioned problems were:

- Books were missing (not on shelf and not checked out) (five responses);
- Insufficient reference assistance on weekends and evenings (four responses);
- Books misshelved (three responses);
- Library should be opened more hours (three responses);
- Staff take longer breaks on weekends and evenings (do not return at the time specified on the signs) (three responses);
- Staff claim to be too busy to provide much help (two responses); and
- Many books await reshelving for long periods of time (two responses).

When asked if the library was service-oriented, 16 (80%) agreed and 2 (10%) agreed strongly. The 2 who disagreed noted bad experiences with reference librarians and the need for more hours of operation. The students' interpretation of service orientation focused on the public service staff with the exception of 1 student, who noted the library always had the material needed. When commenting on public service staff, 10 students mentioned positive attributes (courteous, efficient, and helpful). However, 5 students who agreed the library was service-oriented did mention such problems as rude behavior. One student summed up the negative perception: "I am not unhappy with the library, but enough things are wrong there to make me think that customer satisfaction is not their top priority."

The students were asked to respond to four statements. First, "Service quality is teaching me to be an independent user." Second, "Service quality is providing me with information, books, and articles." Third, "Service quality is both teaching me to be an independent user and providing me with information, books, and articles." And, "Service quality means the library has whatever I need."

For the first statement, responses ranged from 1 ("strongly disagree") to 5 ("strongly agree"), with a mean and median of 4 ("agree"). The mean for the second statement was 4.2000 and the median was 4; for the third statement, the mean was 4.3500 and the median was 4.5000. The final statement's mean was 2.2000 and the median was 2. Clearly, the averages were lowest for the final statement (the library has everything needed) and highest for the third statement (the librarians both teach and provide information).

Table 4.2. Service Quality: Further Revision of the Framework

Resources: Information Content

1. Appropriateness of fit (match) between content and customer
2. Accuracy/trustworthiness
   - Degree of correctness (misinformation)
   - Inaccuracy: Subject to misconduct, (e.g., fraud) (disinformation)
3. Currentness or timeliness
4. Degree of comprehensiveness (e.g., thoroughness and extent to which an electronic product duplicates a print source)
5. Medium
6. Relevance (e.g., information pertinent to the need is available)

The Organization: Its Service Environment and Resource Delivery

1. Availability/accessibility
   - Choices
      - Medium
      - Means of delivery (e.g., fax and OPAC accessible from remote sites via modem)
      - Packaging: Aesthetics (e.g., screen display)
      - Source of service (e.g., which library used, CARL Uncover, or OPAC provides gateway to journal indexes or other library catalogs)
   - Convenience
      - Assistance for electronic services (e.g., help screens, online tutorials, and publicized phone numbers for assistance)
      - Hours of operation
      - Location (e.g., of library or collection)
      - Staffing (service time and availability)—queuing & amount of time for notification of customer of arrival of ILL request, etc.
   - Equipment
      - In operating condition
      - Lines of users waiting their turn
      - More needed
      - Out of order—waiting repair
      - Written/visual instructions correct/not misleading
   - Information itself (ease of its use)
2. Maintenance
   - Items in collection
      - On shelf
      - In proper location (not misshelved/misfiled)
      - No sizable backlog waiting reshelving
      - Length of time item part of backlog (speed of reshelving)
3. Responsiveness, including Complaints/Compliment Procedures
   - Ease of making complaint or compliment
   - Response for receiving good service
   - Response/redress for receiving poor service
4. Physical condition of materials in the collection (e.g., brittle materials or restricted use and photocopying)
5. Physical surroundings
   - Ambient conditions
   - Noisy
   - Personal safety

- Point of public service contact (e.g., branch libraries might have circulation, not reference, desks)
- Signage
- Spatial layout
- Temperature: Too hot/too cold
6. Service costs
7. Service reputation (e.g., as service-oriented)

Service Delivery: Staff [a]

A. Public Service Staff
- Ability to communicate with staff in other units of the library
- Ability to train/educate customers (e.g., in use of CD-ROM products)
- Accuracy in answering questions
- Behavior
    - Approachable
    - Appropriate body language and a smile
    - Courteous
    - Empathetic
    - Friendly/pleasant
    - Include user in search process (i.e., not ignoring his/her presence)
    - Maintain eye contact
    - Not too busy to help: receptivity to being asked a question
    - Willing to leave the desk
- Communication skills
    - Ability to communicate with staff in other units of the library
    - Ability to determine what customer needs
    - Ability to negotiate library system and records (e.g., the library's and other libraries' catalogs and MARC records) to assist customers
    - Conduct reference interview beyond the initial question asked
    - Offer referral
    - Use follow-up question inviting user to return (willingness to return)
- Knowledge
    - Issues (e.g., intellectual property rights)
    - Referral
    - Subject
    - Technical expertise (e.g., formats, accessing electronic information, and Internet access)
- Speed of delivery (mechanical and human)
- Sufficient amount of assistance provided, including the amount of time needed to respond to a request

B. Systems/Technical Service Staff
- Ability to communicate with staff in other units of the library
- Accuracy
- Knowledge of (and ability to anticipate) user needs and information-seeking behavior
- Knowledge of standards
- Service orientation
- Speed of delivery (e.g., in ordering, ILL, and processing)
- Technical knowledge of systems (e.g., technology-based)

[a] In some libraries, staff may perform both public and technical service functions.

When asked if, in addition to the four statements provided, additional attributes of service quality existed, 11 (55%) answered affirmatively. They focused on staff (e.g., courteous, helpful, approachable, friendly, and receptive to questions) and the need for signage.

When asked to identify what they liked most about the library, the students noted convenience of location, the extent of periodical holdings, the fact that the library had multiple copies of most frequently used books, that the periodicals collection does not circulate, free services, interlibrary loans, the friendly attitude of some staff, and that the library is a safe place.

When asked to identify what they liked least, they noted the location of the periodicals area, the library's limited open hours during the weekend, that some materials are held only in distant branch libraries, that a number of books in the collection are outdated, that a number of books and journals are missing or waiting to be reshelved, and the necessity of paying for online services. Some students also commented on unhelpful staff who acted as if they were too busy to provide assistance.

When asked about the "one thing" the library could do to improve itself, responses ranged from placing periodical holdings on the online public access catalog (OPAC), extending weekend hours for the library, providing access to major indexes through the OPAC, creating a smoking section, expanding the circulating collection, changing OPAC printer ribbons more often, making the reference area less cramped, to purchasing more books and journals. A recurring theme was student dissatisfaction with the hours of operation.

Further Pretesting of the First Questionnaire

SITE ONE. At a doctoral-granting institution in the state of Massachusetts that does not have a program in library and information science, seven customers (six undergraduates and one graduate student) and two faculty members, who use the library at least weekly, agreed to participate in a pretest by completing the survey. Eight noted problems with either collections or the physical environment. Regarding the former, they commented on the need for more material in the collection, and for the latter they mentioned the need to reshelve books and bound journals: "Re-shelving seems to be a problem. Often I have noticed books will sit on carts behind the circulation desk for days." They were also likely to comment on the number of copying machines broken and the need for more machines, problems with the heating and cooling system ("It is either too hot or too cold"), or the noise level.

The respondents believed the librarians were service-oriented and they also suggested the survey items adequately conveyed service quality. When asked what they liked most about the library, it was either the friendly and helpful staff or the OPAC. Topping the least-liked list was the collection ("It often does not contain what I need and am looking for"). The typical recommendation for the one thing to do to improve was to purchase more books.

SITE TWO. At a doctoral-granting institution in the state of California that does not have a school of library and information science, we conducted in-person interviews with 12 individuals in the social sciences (three undergraduates, seven graduate students, and two faculty members) who use the library at least once a week. Questions four and five of the survey were rewritten based on their comments.

Ten participants (83.3%) had experienced problems.[2] The most frequently mentioned areas for improvement were collection-related (missing or misshelved items) or service-related (rude staff, especially at the circulation desk, and inadequate hours of staffing public service points in the library). A recurring theme was that "Sometimes I lose faith with the people at circulation who seem to enjoy threatening patrons. However, on the other hand, the interlibrary loan staff are top rate!"

All respondents believed the library had a service orientation; 11 agreed and one did so strongly. When asked what they most liked about the library, they complimented access to an online catalog, the extensive periodicals' holdings, and the interlibrary loan service. They did not appreciate the high level of noise in the library, the rude circulation staff, the library's limited open hours on weekends, and the number of items missing from the collection. As one respondent stated, "I do not like to look up 20 books in...[the OPAC] but only find one in the collection."

When asked to identify the one thing the library could do to improve, the 12 respondents most often mentioned expanding hours of library service, reshelving books faster, reducing noise levels, and eliminating the problem of books missing and misshelved.

Pretesting the Second Questionnaire (Appendix B)

The customers interviewed in the program of library and information science and the California institution did not experience any problems in understanding and completing the *Library Customer Survey*. They did mention, however, that not all the questions applied to their library or, at least, to their use of the library. The librarians concurred with this observation but noted that other applicable statements could be substituted. The users

---

[2] Given the small number of people interviewed, there was no attempt to calculate the mean or median response, or to compare responses by status (student and faculty).

appreciated that the survey did not take long to complete, a fact that they believed would have a positive impact on student participation.

Their responses did not result in any changes to Table 4.2. The table seems to reflect the perspectives of both librarians and customers.

PHASE THREE

Based on phase one responses indicating that it might be possible and beneficial to produce a general list of the most important variables from Table 4.2, we conducted two focus group interviews, one at a northeastern academic library and another at a western one. We asked each of the 12 participants to rank each of the table's component from one (least important) to five (most important), and we then discussed the general findings.

There was no clear agreement on which components were most important; however, respondents did offer some suggestions (see Table 4.3). One participant mentioned some companies expose new staff members to bad service in the hope that they will benefit from that experience. Nonetheless, under "behavior," the broadest consensus concerned approachable and

Table 4.3. Most Important Variables: Some Suggestions [a]

Resources: Information Content

Accuracy/trustworthiness
Appropriateness of fit (match) between content and customer

The Organization

Availability/accessibility
Equipment (in operating order)

Service Delivery

A. Public service staff
    Ability to train/educate customers
    Accuracy in answering questions
    Behavior: Approachable and Courteous
    Communication skills: Ability to determine what customer needs
B. Systems/technical service staff
    Ability to communicate with staff in other units of the library
    Accuracy
    Knowledge of (and ability to anticipate) user needs and information-seeking behavior
    Service orientation

[a] The suggestions identified here received votes from five to six participants. No suggestions received more than six votes.

courteous behavior, which received the most votes.

The participants questioned the extent to which they would be willing to rely on insights gained from the use of self-reporting. For example, a few asked, "What if customers want the library to expand the hours of operation and we do, but then there is no increased use?" In effect, as one noted, "We could adapt the famous statement from the movie *Field of Dreams* so that it becomes a question: 'If we build it, will they come?'" This concern is a reminder that our research must offer more than self-reporting techniques as a basis for data collection, planning, and decision making.

Given the nature of the findings, the remaining two phases of this investigation abandoned the attempt to identify the most important variables that might be common across libraries and institutions.

PHASE FOUR

During this phase, three academic libraries, all affiliated with doctoral-granting institutions, agreed to administer the pretested questionnaires to their customers. The data collected were used to review, once more, Table 4.2 and service quality. Survey responses did produce one change to the table. Respondents complained about the building being either too hot or too cold; therefore, we added "temperature" to the "The Organization."

We also shared Table 4.2 with the library staff of a community college system and a baccalaureate-granting institution. Both staffs certified the components of the table as comprehensive.

Questionnaire One

Over a two-day period during final-examination week, reference staff members at one library got 50 completed questionnaires from undergraduate (32 or 64%) and graduate (16 or 32%) students, and faculty members (2 or 4%). Thirty (60%) of them use the library at least once a week; 20 (40%) use it a few times per month.

On the whole, the respondents had nothing but praise for the library and its staff. Typically, they remarked on the "helpful staff who go out of their way to provide assistance." One student wanted the library to "run a campaign and get popular support to increase the budget, even if it means taking money away from SPORTS!" Only four (8%) noted any problems related to collections, physical environment, or services. Mostly, they commented on the length of time that items were in the bindery, the building was too cold, or the fact that find items listed in the OPAC were not available.

In response to the statement that the library is service-oriented, they concurred: the mean was 4.20 and the median was 4. Service quality was mostly viewed as "teaching me to be an independent user" (mean, 4.14; median, 4), followed by "handing me information and/or sources" and "both teaching me to be an independent user and handing me information and/or sources" (both statements produced a mean of 4.02 and median of 4). The final statement, "The library, always or most often, has whatever I need," generated a mean of 3.94 and median of 4.

When asked if there were other attributes of service quality in addition to those depicted in the previous statements, 14 (28%) stated "yes." They focused predominantly on a "friendly" and "knowledgeable" staff "eager to assist."

When asked about what they liked *most* about the library, respondents commented on the OPAC, the large collection of books and periodicals, the helpful staff, ample study areas that are quiet, and materials that are easily accessible. They liked *least* the noise and that the temperature in the library was either too hot or too cold. The one improvement that they were most likely to mention was adjustment in the temperature. A number of respondents expressed their comfort with technology and wanted to see the library expand its holdings of CD-ROM and provide more printers for the computers.

In summary, this questionnaire was designed to provide feedback to the framework on service quality (Table 4.2). Thus, libraries wanting to use this questionnaire undoubtedly would delete or revise questions four and five.

Questionnaire Two

SITE ONE. At the one academic library, library users (either ones in the stacks or sitting at tables) were approached and asked to participate. Only a few declined; they did so primarily due to time constraints. One hundred, however, did participate in the study. There were 60 undergraduate (60%) and 40 graduate (40%) students.

Table 4.4 summarizes the mean and median responses to the 25 statements, which respondents could have answered on a scale of 1 to 5, where 1 was "no importance" and 5 was "highest importance." Eight statements produced a mean of at least 4 and a median of 5. These statements group into four categories:

- ➤ Accuracy: of answers to questions about library materials and the contents of library materials;
- ➤ Maintenance: prompt reshelving, material in proper location, online catalog recording if material is checked out, and the library having what the person is searching for;
- ➤ Safety on the premises; and
- ➤ Equipment in working condition.

The nature of the responses suggests that those adapting the questionnaire to fit their own situations and data-collection needs might add "no opinion" as an occasional option (only where relevant and where it would be inappropriate to try to force a choice); also, the situation may arise in which more

Table 4.4. Responses to Customer Survey

	Mean	Median
The staff answer your questions about library materials accurately	4.48	5
The information you get from library books and periodicals is accurate	4.46	5
Books and journals are reshelved promptly	4.40	5
The materials you want are in their proper places on the shelves	4.36	5
The computerized catalog indicates if materials are checked out or are in the library	4.33	5
The library has the current books and journals you are searching for	4.32	5
You feel safe in the building	4.26	5
Equipment such as terminals, photocopiers, and printers are in operating condition	4.23	5 [a]
The library is open late at night and for long hours on the weekend	4.13	4.50
The staff help you find information you need	4.19	4
Each floor or major area of the library has terminals in working condition to access the online catalog	4.19	4
The restrooms and drinking fountains are clean	4.10	4
Library staff understand the information for which you are looking	4.09	4
The library staff are friendly	4.03	4
Study areas are quiet	4.02	4
You do not have to wait more than a few minutes for service	3.89	4
You can print off the information about call numbers or journal articles appearing on the computer screens	3.87	4
It is easy to find where books, journals and other types of library materials are located in the building	3.83	4
It is clear where help may be found when you are having a problem finding materials or using equipment in the library	3.82	4

Staff help you to use the electronic catalog and indexes	3.82	4
Staff suggest that you can obtain materials that the library does not own by using interlibrary loan	3.59	4 [b]
You can renew or request material via the online catalog	3.43	3.50 [c]
You can access the online catalog via modem from your home	3.43	3 [c]
Staff are available on each floor of the building to answer questions about finding materials	3.23	3
Staff take you where the material is shelved instead of just pointing or telling you where to go	3.04	3

[a] There were four missing responses. It might be useful to subdivide this question into several questions. For example, one question looks at photocopiers, another examines printers, etc. See Chapter 7.
[b] There were five missing responses, indicating the need to rewrite the question. Appendix B contains the rewritten question as does Chapter 7.
[c] There were six missing responses. Appendix B contains the rewritten question in one case. Also see Chapter 7.

descriptive variables, such as gender, could be added. With a larger sample of data and the inclusion of more variables, it would be possible to engage in hypothesis testing and to use statistical tests such as the chi-square test of independence. As previously mentioned, other statements might be substituted. Still, it is essential to conduct a pretest and ensure reliability of the wording.

SITE TWO. Like the other site, this was a doctoral-granting institution. Every tenth customer of one service area was selected and the number of completed surveys totaled 70. The purpose of this pilot project was also to review Table 4.2 and to revise the survey form as necessary.

Table 4.5 identifies the mean and median for each of the 25 statements. A comparison of Tables 4.4 and 4.5 indicates differences among the respondents at both institutions. As discussed in the next chapter, valid insights probably require more completed surveys. Nonetheless, the 170 responses from the two institutions reveal interesting information.

At the second site, the customers want to be able to find what they are searching for. They also want material in the proper location and to know the status of the material (checked out or likely on the shelves). At the next tier of responses, they want a safe building. One respondent wrote on the back of the survey:

Until recently I felt very safe in the library. As of late, however, an elderly woman has taken up residence on the first floor. She often solicits money. This is very disturbing to those of us trying to study. I suspect the woman is homeless but she should be removed at once. For $25,000 a year, students deserve to be left in peace.

In comparison to the other site, accuracy was less important (not unimportant) as was equipment in working order. If we collapse responses for both sites into one list, the six most important statements are:

- The staff answer your questions about library materials accurately (mean, 4.39; median, 5);
- The materials you want are in their proper places on the shelves (mean, 4.36; median 5);
- The library has the current books and journals you want or are searching for (mean, 4.35; median, 5);
- The information you get from library books and periodicals is accurate (mean, 4.33; median, 5);
- The computerized catalog indicates if materials are checked out or in the library (mean, 4.33; median, 5); and
- You feel safe in the building (mean, 4.30; median, 5).

As this section illustrates, service quality varies according to the local situation. With a larger response rate, differences among customer groups might emerge and priorities might shift. Still, the responses indicate that customers do not have neutral perceptions on any of the 25 statements.

Table 4.5. Further Responses to Customer Survey

	Mean	Median
The library has the current books and journals you are searching for	4.38	5
The materials you want are in their proper places on the shelves	4.37	5
The computerized catalog indicates if materials are checked out or are in the library	4.36	5
You feel safe in the building	4.34	4.50
Each floor or major area of the library has terminals in working condition to access the online catalog	4.31	4
The staff answer your questions about library materials accurately	4.27	4
The staff help you find information you need	4.24	4
The information you get from library books and periodicals is accurate	4.15	4

The library staff are friendly	4.13	4
Library staff understand the information for which you are looking	4.11	4
The library is open late at night and for long hours on the weekend	4.06	4
The restrooms and drinking fountains are clean	4.04	4
Equipment such as terminals, photocopiers, and printers is in operating condition	4.03	4
It is clear where help may be found when you are having a problem finding materials or using equipment in the library	4.01	4
It is easy to find where books, journals, and other types of library materials are located in the building	3.94	4
Staff help you to use the electronic catalog and indexes	3.93	4
Books and journals are reshelved promptly	3.93	4
Study areas are quiet	3.90	4
You can print off the information about call numbers or journal articles appearing the computer screens	3.84	4
You do not have to wait more than a few minutes for service	3.81	4
Staff obtain materials that the library does not own	3.79	4
You can renew or request materials via the online catalog	3.56	4 [a]
You can access the online catalog via modem from your home	3.41	4
Staff are available on each floor of the building to answer questions about finding materials	3.40	3
Staff take you to where the material is shelved instead of just pointing or telling you where to go	3.25	3

[a] There were six missing cases. One other statement had four missing cases and the others had 0, 1, or 2 missing cases.

PHASE FIVE

At the AMIGOS conference in Dallas, Texas, in May 1995, we gave the keynote address on service quality and provided a general overview of the findings presented in this chapter. A panel of three administrators (one from an academic library, one from a public library, and the other from a special library) responded as did the audience of approximately 190 librarians. There is definite interest in the application of service quality to academic and public libraries, and strong interest in the major findings from this study. In effect, there is a hunger for ways to depict the quality of services to those to whom library directors report, and to justify the library's budgetary needs and decisions. Nonetheless, librarians are still searching for the magic key to unlock the treasure chest full of money for collections, services, and operations. They wanted one-stop shopping or one data collection that will meet any and all of their needs. Some in the audience wondered if our approach to service quality would provide them with sufficient evidence to compare themselves to peer institutions and, at the same time, demonstrate internal effectiveness to higher education administrators, while simultaneously being a simple and convenient way to gather that evidence.

Despite our inability to fulfill such expectations, they acknowledged that our approach and intent to provide managerial data relating to service quality was an important starting point. They suggested that future focus groups might include library paraprofessional staff, and that the approaches ultimately discussed in Chapter 7 offer important ways to complement or replace the use of surveys and focus group interviews. They agreed they received "a lot of food for thought" and said widespread "legitimation" or adoption of the processes for improvement discussed in this chapter and the next three would require endorsements from organizations such as the Association of Research Libraries, the Association of College and Research Libraries, and the Council of Library Resources. The unresolved question from discussions which we overheard outside the one session is: "Where do we go from this first step taken by the research reported...[here]?" Of course, this question is not for us or this book to answer.

CONCLUSION

Customers—faculty, staff, students, and others—have different expectations and librarians cannot meet each one. However, they can meet some and explain why others cannot be resolved, and thereby improve library services and maintain an active dialogue with customers. Furthermore, as the chapter illustrates, there are many components to service quality. Libraries must determine which ones are the most relevant to their situation, and concentrate on meeting them. Clearly, service quality is more appropriately viewed as an internal matter—that is, encompassing the needs and uniqueness of the local organization—than as a basis of comparison to other institutions. Finally, service quality defines libraries as systems in which the entire organization works toward the accomplishment of common goals.

Chapter 5

Surveying Customers

Service providers must continually challenge themselves to improve their products and develop new innovations.

—Gorchels, 1995, p. 503

Your ability to provide high-quality service to the customer is going to be highly dependent on your ability to interpret what the customer wants and to respond with the appropriate actions.

—LoSardo & Rossi, 1993, p. 46

The librarians participating in the focus group interviews for Chapter 4 reported they wanted the opportunity to select from Table 4.2 those components of service quality most appropriate to their own situation. Moreover, the procedures for collecting and analyzing the data gathered must be convenient and easy to implement. They made it clear they were busy and regarded any data collection as adding to their already extensive list of responsibilities. Although we did not introduce the topic of redesigning job-related duties and responsibilities in order to work more efficiently, there is clearly the need to do so. As the focus group participants realized, service quality raises important issues that should not be ignored or for which librarians should not assume they are doing all that they can.

The participants endorsed the development and adoption of a practical approach to data collection and to the creation of standardized procedures. The purpose of this chapter is to provide a basis from which librarians can modify either or both data collection instruments (Appendices A and B) to meet their local needs.

This chapter explains key concepts and discusses how to conduct a survey of in-house users or of the larger community. As more libraries question the extent to which the entire academic community uses the library and the patterns of their use, libraries will want to consider procedures that can be generalized. However, they should not exclude approaches that are specific. Service quality focuses on current users and attempts to ensure that they remain customers. Libraries can also seek potential customers—new ones or those previously dissatisfied and relying on other service organizations—and meet more of their service expectations.

The focus of the chapter is on data collection that produces useful insights but is not costly to do. That data collection might involve the use of quantitative or qualitative methods, or the use of both techniques.

DATA COLLECTION INSTRUMENTS

The librarians participating in the focus group interviews showed the most interest in the application of the *Library Customer Survey* (reprinted in Appendix B). As mentioned in the previous chapter, using Table 4.2, librarians can review the 25 statements, adding, deleting, or modifying them. They might add statements about use of the reserve collection, the mutilation of library resources, or specific types of equipment.

The *Library Customer Survey* contains easy to answer statements and does not take long to complete. Because the survey is short, librarians might include some questions from the other survey, *Service Quality for Library Users* (see Appendix A), in particular, questions about what customers like most and least about the library, and what one thing would they recommend for improvement. The resulting two-page questionnaire probes many aspects of service quality.

In analyzing the survey data reported in the previous chapter, we used StatPac Gold (see Hernon, 1994b), a statistical analysis software package for microcomputers. As an alternative, librarians might use spreadsheet (e.g., Lotus, Excel, or Quarto Pro) or data management (e.g., dBase, Paradox, or Symphony) software. By reducing the data collection form to one page and asking a maximum of 10 statements, they might purchase and use Benevox™, the software package discussed in Chapter 3.

STATISTICAL ANALYSIS

Statistical analysis software would produce the mean and median for each statement (like we did in the previous chapter). Depending on the background variables included—such as gender, status (faculty or student), age, part-time or full-time position, and frequency of library use—they might also generate percentages and use cross-tabulation to compare one nominal or ordinal variable to another (see Hernon, 1994b, Chapters 5 and 7).

The Benevox scale for statements is one to 10, with numbers grouped to produce interval-level data characterized by the mean. Thus, our statements with the range of one to five are easily converted to the Benevox scale.

For open-ended questions asking what customers liked most and least, the entire responses can be entered into the software. The software for open-ended questions merely reproduces a list of responses. Any pulling together of like responses would require hand tabulation or use of another software package.

It is also possible to convert the open-ended questions into questions in which respondents select from among a menu of choices. The menu might be selective and avoid the use of the "other" option. The purpose of doing so is to attempt to force respondents to make choices from a specific list of options.

SAMPLING

Librarians who have considered or applied output measures as discussed in Van House et al. (1987) and Van House, Weil, and McClure (1990) have been exposed to sampling. Instead of viewing a population, they deal with a portion of it. *Sampling method* refers to the type of sampling procedure chosen to study that portion. The purpose of probability sampling is to make a statistical inference or to select a sample that is representative of the population. Probability sampling includes, for instance, simple random sampling, stratified random sampling, systematic sampling, and cluster sampling (see Powell, 1991). Nonprobability sampling does not support generalization; rather, the focus is on the sample itself. Nonprobability sampling is discretionary and covers quota sampling, purposive or judgmental sampling, convenience sampling, and other methods (see Powell, 1991). In effect, the individuals chosen are convenient or expedient to reach, or they might be selected for a particular purpose; for instance, they might be considered typical or representative, or they might comprise an extreme, best, or worst case. Librarians might want to select, for example, only frequent users of the OPAC, users of electronic services, or students who had previously completed a library instruction program or course.

As becomes evident, with probability sampling, there is interest in generalizing findings to a population, whereas the purpose for selecting a nonprobability sample differs. Librarians are often less interested in generalization; they want to examine individuals with certain characteristics: they are regular library users, they belong to a particular college or class level, or so forth.

Sampling Method

Librarians might consider the use of either a simple random sample or a systematic sample. The former involves the selection of cases or subjects so that each one has an equal and known chance of inclusion and the selection of one case or subject does not influence the selection of another. For the latter type, researchers or evaluators select the *nth* subject; they predetermine that *nth* is, say, every 20th person entering the library or using reference or circulation desk services. In part, the determination of which sampling method to use depends on the number of staff assigned to the distribution, explanation, and collection of survey forms.

As an alternative, librarians might use a nonprobability sample, such as a quota sample, in which they predetermine that they want to study the perceptions of upper division undergraduates majoring in the social sciences. In such a case, they might query students entering the library about their status and select those meeting the above-mentioned characteristics. They would also have decided on the number of completed survey forms they want to gather and then distribute the forms until they achieve their quota.

Sample Size

Librarians considering the use of probability sampling should review Hernon (1994a) for the discussion of how to determine sample size. The article identifies different concepts to address and both print sources and software useful in determining the size of a simple random or proportional sample.

One easy-to-use, menu-driven software package is *Dr. Drott's Random Sampler* (Drott, 1993). The accompanying 77-page manual contains examples of determining a simple random sample or basing sample selection on weeks of the year, days of the week, hours of the day, and minutes of the hour. The manual clearly explains the concepts necessary to draw a random sample, and the software allows researchers to adjust sample size to population size.

Table 6.1 of Hernon (1994b, p. 121) identifies different sample sizes for a confidence of 95 percent and precision of plus or minus 5, and Table 6.2 of the same source (p. 122) shows the sample sizes for a confidence of 90 percent and a precision of plus or minus 5. Using the first table, librarians might determine they want a sample size of 207. Turning to a table of random numbers or a statistical software package, such as StatPac, they could select the actual participants. As an alternative, they might use a systematic sampling technique to choose the participants.

Table 5.1. Sample Questions Guiding Data Collection

- Has approval from the library administration and human subjects committee been granted?
- Who will be in charge of data collection?
- What resources will the person(s) have?
- When will data collection be done?
- How can we assure that staff members do not feel threatened by data collection?
- How will the data be analyzed and used?
- What type of sampling method will be used?
- Do the librarians want to focus on particular groups?
- How big of a sample will be used?
- How will participants be selected?
- What do librarians want to ask on the survey?
- Did respondents follow directions and complete all questions?
- Where will the survey be administered, at particular service points or the entrance/exit to the library?
- Where should completed questionnaires be returned?

PROCEDURES

As we experienced at one library, use of the survey required clearance from the institution's review committee on human subjects. Such a process protects the welfare and confidentiality of respondents. Thus, librarians should determine if the institution has such a committee and should seek approval. The committee might also require certain actions, such as signage explaining the project and voluntary participation. Table 5.1 identifies other questions librarians should answer as they prepare to use either a quantitative or qualitative method.

Both survey instruments were inexpensive to develop and distribute. Furthermore, users of the three libraries were willing to participate; there was little refusal. Librarians at the three institutions approached data collection with a positive attitude and realized that, although it was not our direct intention, the findings had value to them. We easily could have had many more respondents to the three surveys; however, it was our primary intention to review Table 4.2 and conduct pilot studies.

Survey

The librarians might conduct a mailed or telephone survey, or place the survey in the student newspaper or on e-mail, but more likely they will conduct a study of in-house users, such as we did in Chapter 4.

Measuring Academic Library Performance (Van House, Weil, & McClure, 1990), although focusing on an entirely different set of measures and method of evaluation, does represent a manual that had extensive involvement from academic libraries and the Association of College and Research Libraries. Of course, our research has been conducted on a much more modest scale and, therefore, we can only provide general guidance to libraries wanting to use our data collection forms. At this stage of our research, we recommend that librarians review *Measuring Academic Library Performance* and points such as "preparing the staff" (pp. 27–28):

- The entire staff, including those not directly concerned with the survey, should be informed of the purpose of the survey and the procedures. Staff throughout the library are likely to be questioned by users ("Why are you asking all these questions?" "How do I answer this question?" "Where do I return the questionnaire?"). They should know the answers or to whom to refer questions. (p. 27)
- Staff may feel threatened by any measurement, fearing that they individually are the targets of evaluation... The more that they understand, the less threatened staff members will be. (p. 27)
- Finally, staff may have practical suggestions about how to make the survey process run smoothly. (p. 27)

Measuring Academic Library Performance discusses "deciding how many questionnaires to distribute" (p. 28) and, for the General Satisfaction Survey, Van House, Weil, and McClure (1990) recommend: "In most cases, you will need at least 100 completed forms; closer to 400 is preferable. Users are generally quite cooperative; response rates of 80 to 90 percent on the General Satisfaction Survey are common" (p. 44). Librarians might experiment with their suggestions about the number of completed forms or pursue a random sample with a certain confidence and precision.

Next, they should choose either the *Service Quality for Library Users* (Appendix A) or the *Library Customer Survey* (Appendix B), and review and revise it as necessary. Once they have done this, they might gather students employed by the library and involve them in a pretest, reviewing the wording of the questions (or statements) and determining whether they are asking what they want to know. The pretest might also review options for distributing questionnaires and ensuring the highest possible rate of return, and involve a brief field test of the survey. Again, Van House, Weil, and McClure (1990) offer useful advice:

In some libraries it works best to give questionnaires to users as they leave. The questionnaire only takes a minute, and you avoid the danger of users losing them in the library or forgetting to fill them out. In some libraries, however, users on their way out of the library are reluctant to stop for any reason, and you should give them questionnaires as they enter. Try both approaches during your pretest, and choose one. (pp. 44, 46)

Once data have been collected and managerial decisions made, any major changes in service should be publicized. The purpose is to demonstrate that the librarians value and profit from the comments. If customers see their comments make a difference, they will be more willing to cooperate in the future. After all, service quality involves ongoing and continuous assessment.

Focus Group Interviews

Glazier and Powell (1992) noted that qualitative research methods view:

Experiences from the perspective of those involved and attempt to understand why individuals react or behave as they do. They tend to give more attention to the subjective aspects of human experience and behavior. In short, qualitative research takes a more natural approach to the resolution of research problems. (p. xi)

Researchers often use focus group interviews as a means of qualitative research or the production of findings not necessarily reduced to measurement (see Chapter 2).[1] Typically 6 to 10 people come together and provide information on highly focused issues or problems. Group members interact and the researcher or an independent party assumes the role of impartial moderator (see Krueger, 1988; Morgan, 1988).

For a focus group interview, librarians must therefore decide on whom to invite and who should serve as an impartial moderator. Before conducting an interview, the librarian(s) coordinating the session must meet with the moderator and explain the context of the interview and what the staff want to accomplish. The moderator must receive the five to seven questions to ask and be given an opportunity to ask about the intent of each question.

During the interview, the moderator might summarize responses to ensure that there is common agreement on what has transpired. Also, upon conclusion of the interview, the moderator or someone else produces a transcript of the discussion. A summary of the interview might be given to the participants to see if there is anything to add, change, or upon which to expand.

---

[1] Van House et al. (1987, p. 1) define measurement as the collection, analysis, and organization of objective, quantitative data. In effect, researchers reduce interpretation of the dataset to numbers. Focus group interviews, on the other hand, typically avoid precise measurement.

CONCLUSION

Upon completion of the fourth phase reported in the previous chapter—reviewing the conceptual framework for service quality and involving the general administration of the two surveys, we conduced two focus group interviews at a southern university library. The 14 participants believed we had collected data useful for better meeting the needs of customers. However, some were skeptical about two findings from Chapter 4: (a) students calling for expanded hours of opening and staffing the library, and (b) the extent to which items were indeed misshelved. They questioned whether students would, in fact, take advantage of extended hours or services, and they suspected that the problem might be less misshelving and more student inability to negotiate a classification scheme to find material on the shelves.

When asked if students at their institution might issue similar complaints, they surmised that they might. They mentioned problems related to the hiring and retaining of good student shelvers, and they noted during busy times during the semester the problems of misshelving materials and the backlog of books and journals waiting reshelving became worse. Items, they mentioned, might wait four to five days before being reshelved.[2] They understood that whether the problem relates to misshelving or student inability to negotiate the collection, failure to resolve whichever one accounted for the problem directly impacts service quality. It can be useful to develop data collection techniques that focus on areas needing improvement rather than presumed successes (e.g., measures of satisfaction and output measures).

Service quality might be a potential problem at this library. Although some of the librarians rationalized the status quo—why they cannot reduce the amount of time for reshelving or lessening the extent of misshelved material, they realized that multi-method research, such as following the survey with selected focus group interviews, provides a mechanism for placing survey responses in perspective and pursuing methods for correcting problems.

Multi-method research directed at better managing the library and better serving library customers becomes useful. The managers, however, might not want to engage in the type of surveying discussed in this chapter and the previous one. They might also want to explore other facets of service quality and go beyond self-reported data. To this end, Chapter 6 and 7 offer other choices for investigating the various facets of Table 4.2. It merits repeating that the intent of evaluation and data collection is not to lay blame but to seek improvement.

---

[2] The shelvers at Memphis/Shelby County (Tennessee) Public Library work the night shift to reshelve materials and transport items for intralibrary loan. By 9 a.m., all materials from the previous day have be reshelved.

Chapter 6

Creating a
Service Quality
Information System

---

*The next time I go to the hospital, I'd rather see a Baldrige Award on the wall
than a Harvard diploma.*

—Mackay (1995, p. E6)

According to Seymour (1995, p. 80), most college campuses are "awash in data but thirsty for information." The same could be said about their libraries. Most functional departments conscientiously keep statistics which are duly reported to unit managers who pass them up the line to the library's top administrators. These statistics generally reflect work completed by the unit: the number of items ordered, the number of items given original cataloging, the number of serials checked in, and the number of reference questions asked. Businesses call such data "bundles over the wall." The expectation is that others will be there to catch the bundle and do with it what they will, with the compilers neither knowing nor really caring ("Customer Service Data," 1995, p. 16).

Other than indicating the staff is working, what does the information prove? It does not tell how effectively or efficiently staff members are working: Could they have processed more items, completed their work faster, or done something more important for improving customer service? Furthermore, each unit's numbers stand in isolation; there is no way to assess how the reported activities contribute to the totality of library service.

Does any of this information reflect customers' satisfaction or frustrations? Does this information tell how well any of these units facilitated or hindered customer access to information, or are these reports merely "a ritualistic exercise...providing answers to questions that no one is asking" (Seymour, 1995, p. 80)? An information system that give managers a realistic picture of how (and how well) the library serves its customers is needed. That information system should focus on those elements important to customers, and should illustrate how the library might improve both quality and productivity to meet customer expectations. For example, most libraries keep some count of reference transactions (the number of questions asked by customers). Would it not be of interest to know how many customers left public service areas because the lines were too long, or because they could not find staff available to help?

DON'T HAVE THE TIME OR STAFF

Frequent excuses for not collecting more, or different, data about service are lack of time or staff or both. Such rationales imply either that current processes, policies, and work by the staff are all as efficient and effective as possible (a highly dubious assumption), or that the administration simply does not place a high priority on customer service.

All of us have opinions about our own work and work places, but those opinions are usually unsupported by hard evidence. By identifying and quantifying the *facts* relating to each process or service point, we get the whole picture of what needs to be done, and what can be eliminated. (For example, many academic librarians bemoan the amount of time spent in meetings. Is the time spent worth the time lost?)

Harry Forsha (1992), a businessman who believes that to improve customer service we must first improve ourselves, said, "Numerical data are facts that are hard to refute and make a powerful weapon in the war against denial" (p. 11). Most librarians would deny they offer substandard service, but they really know very little about the quality of their service because they have not analyzed the service elements from the customers' perspectives.

The economic conditions of the 1990s have resulted in either freezing or eliminating positions in some libraries. Such circumstances demand those libraries to rethink both their priorities and their processes to ensure that the things most important to customers are the ones getting attention. Cutbacks offer an opportune time to think about what no longer needs to be done. Every organization makes trade-offs between cost and service; however, the trick is to redeploy cost so as not to diminish seriously service quality.

IT ALL STARTS AT THE TOP

Library staff will not focus on service quality or customer expectations until they are convinced the top administrators are seriously committed to those concepts. Staff clearly understand that the administrators, not the customers, hold the power to reward or sanction them. Until customer service becomes a major element in the reward system, staff will conduct business as usual to stay within their individual comfort zones.

Casey Stengel, legendary manager of the New York Yankees and later the New York Mets, once remarked, "You can learn a lot by just watching." Whether they know Stengel's observation or not, successful managers do watch what is happening. They get out of their offices and walk around. They see for themselves what is happening and talk to customers. Robert Townsend (1970), former president of Avis, frequently called Avis offices pretending to be a customer so he could experience firsthand the way that employees treated customers. When is the last time the head of public services personally checked out a book on a weekend? When did the head of reference last phone in a reference question?

The attitude of the library administration toward service clearly filters down to the staff who will generally (or begrudgingly) do whatever the administration emphasizes. If there is minimal emphasis on customer service, then service suffers. Staff reaction to customers will be, "It's not my job." Worse yet, they may blame customers for causing service problems, such as when too many of them arrive during the noon hour, creating long lines at service points. It is not fair for staff to complain, "But it is the staff lunch hour." Wendy's, the fast food chain, and many banks, on the other hand, put on more, not fewer, staff on duty at noontime.

SERVICE FAILURES PRESENT OPPORTUNITIES

Traditionally, most reporting systems in education and libraries focus on accomplishments (e.g., the number of graduates by level of degree or the number of titles circulated) as perceived organizational successes. However, knowing the organization's shortcomings may be more helpful both to administrators and staff because recognizing the organization's shortcomings, or the shortcomings of any of its component parts, is the first step to improving customer service. Typical reports submitted by unit managers to the library director or dean emphasize the good things, especially the number of items processed (considered to be a good thing) by their staffs during the previous year. No manager wants to tell the supervisor bad news. Usually unit managers will admit to problems only to underscore the need for more staff or more equipment, or to seek relief from some tasks deemed onerous for that unit. However, once unit managers understand that reporting the not-so-good things is permissible as long as the situation improves, the first step in service quality will be taken.

Typically, the problems that disappoint or frustrate customers are the unavailability of wanted materials, inoperable equipment, difficulty in understanding how the library and its materials are organized, and inept, unresponsive, and condescending staff. The causes of many of these problems can be traced to bottlenecks, waste, and the failure to understand or acknowledge customer expectations and customer behaviors. The best way to identify the bottlenecks, waste, and unmet expectations is to listen to the customers. Other causes of customer dissatisfaction include improper assignment of staff (e.g., having only student workers at the reference desk), inadequate training for regular staff, and failure to delineate expectations for staff performance. However, many service failures can be the impetus for ultimately improving customer service if the library will give the customers a voice to articulate what they want from the service and if the library will try to solve customer problems as they arise before they become resentments told far and wide.

GIVE THE CUSTOMERS A VOICE

How attuned are library decision makers to their customers' feelings about the service they receive? For example, can librarians answer the following questions with confidence:

- What do customers like best about the service?
- What problems do customers encounter most frequently?
- What processes should be corrected to benefit the customer? (adapted from Hinton & Schaeffer, 1994, p. 35)

Suggestion boxes (either print or electronic), if they are properly used, provide invaluable insights into service quality. Proper use means taking the suggestions seriously, not just ignoring them or making excuses about why suggestions cannot be implemented or problems fixed. One element of proper use is to categorize the suggestions for analysis. Brown (1994) described categories at Wichita State University. These included:

- Buildings and facilities;
- Library policies;
- Finding tools; and
- Ways to make things easier for patrons. (p. 215)

Customers deserve responses to their suggestions. These can be posted on a bulletin board (again, either print or electronic, or both) for anyone to read, and perhaps to entice others to suggest enhancements to the basic suggestions. We are not recommending that library managers follow all suggestions such as those for coffee bars, food service, and smoking rooms. However, suggestions likely to improve information service in the broadest context should be carefully considered.

HOW MANY PROBLEMS BECOME COMPLAINTS?

Most dissatisfied customers do not complain. Only about five percent of those who do go to the top administrators with their complaints. Another, somewhat larger, group complains to front-line staff. Why do so few people complain? The answer is either there is no obvious channel for complaints or they believe no one in the organization really cares.

Service quality can be described as the relationship between customer expectations of service and the actual service delivered; therefore, how a library responds to the gap between the two is a reflection of its commitment to quality. "Libraries tend to be very bureaucratic in organization...especially in larger facilities...people tend to be very compartmentalized...The rigid organizational structure discourages—if not actually forbids —stepping outside their assigned role" (Barter, 1994, p. 10).

What happens when a customer speaks to a staff member (including student workers) about a problem in the library? Are staff instructed how to respond, or do they believe that they have no authority or responsibility to solve the problem? Responses such as "I'm sorry," "I can't do anything," or merely shrugging, are indicative of an organization that does not care about its customers. An even worse reaction to a problem is defensiveness by the staff member or the administration. (If the library or an employee is at fault, then employees should have the grace to admit error.) Research conducted in many different types of organizations shows dissatisfied customers tell twice as many people about their experiences than do satisfied customers ("Making Complaints Pay," 1994). Unhappy customers usually do not return to places where they perceive unsatisfactory service. Customers of academic libraries are usually, at least, a "semi-captive" audience; they may not have many alternatives—yet. However, this is no excuse for adopting the line from the old comedy show in which the switchboard operator said, "We don't care; we don't have to care. We're the phone company." Look what happened to Bell Telephone as a result of such an attitude!

Good managers want to hear about problems, which enable them to pinpoint areas needing improvement. To that end, they let all employees know that complaints and requests for assistance are welcome and even encouraged. Every employee should be trained regarding both attitude and procedures for handling complaints, and all regular employees should know they have both the authority and the responsibility to try to solve the customer's problem at the time it is presented. Student employees should have a regular staff member available to whom they can refer customers with problems. Organizations that leave departments totally in the care of student workers do not care about customers.

Does the library have forms for registering complaints? What happens after the complaint is received? The library's response says a lot about its commitment to service quality. An insincere apology is perceived as such. Some letters responding to complaints annoy the customer even further. One such letter, written by a library director in response to a complaint about poor service that was subsequently published in the university newspaper, apologized tepidly but noted the complainant was not a member of the academic community. The letter implied that it was, therefore, a special privilege to have use of the university library at all.

Customers want to know that action will be taken as the result of their complaint. A phone call in response is often better than a letter to show that the top people really care about keeping customers satisfied. Although complaint forms are better than no formal mechanism for dealing with problems, they are less than responsive because they do not deal with the problem in time to help the customer. Thus, all the customer gets is an apology and a half-hearted promise to try to do better in the future. Neither of these gets to the issue of service quality. Complaints stem from two causes—perceived poor service or lack of service. Library managers must identify the causes of complaints and fix them rather than treating each complaint as a unique, and thus ignorable, event. It should be every library manager's goal never to get the same complaint twice.

RATIONALE FOR A SERVICE QUALITY
INFORMATION SYSTEM (SQIS)

"As we begin to reengineer our library organizations, our focus must be user centered or we will find ourselves in the business of managing a warehouse of old information rather than being in the forefront of providing information" (Shapiro & Long, 1994, p. 286). We tried to adhere to that advice as we developed measures to provide unit managers and administrators with information about service quality in their libraries. We used the following criteria in developing the system:

- It must cover the entire range of items important to customers, including both the physical aspects of the building and collections as well as the attitude and competence of the staff.

- Individual aspects of service must reflect the priorities of customers, not librarians. (For example, the quality of catalog records is seldom of high priority to most customers.)
- Data must be relatively easy to collect in terms of time and effort.
- Data analysis and interpretation must be straightforward.
- The information collected must be relevant for decision making.

The elements of the Service Quality Information System (SQIS) were developed during a series of focus groups with librarians at different academic libraries (see Chapter 4). We fleshed out broad areas such as "accessibility" and delineated individual facets relative to service, such as hours of operation, access to equipment in working condition, and access to the building. We also used the list to create two separate questionnaires that were distributed to customers in some university libraries (see Chapter 4 and Appendices A and B).

The responses to the focus group and survey questions identified other items important to customers. For example, we had not previously considered customers' concerns about physical safety in the library as an item of importance until it was mentioned in responses to the first questionnaire. As a result, the second questionnaire specifically asked if "physical safety in the library" was important to customers, and, indeed, it ranked high among most of the respondents. Ultimately, we developed a list of items, shown in Table 6.1, that satisfied the criteria of broad inclusion and importance to library customers.

Our intent is to make data collection as simple as possible. Data about service quality measures in the SQIS can be collected by checklist, from the telephone company, from online public access catalog (OPAC) statistics, by camcorder, by measurement of response time, by customer focus groups, by online surveys, or by surrogate customers (e.g., the trained shoppers businesses use to monitor service). Most data for the measures can be collected with a minimum of time and effort. Individual libraries can pick and choose which elements of service they want to assess. In many cases, the service quality measures are not dependent upon each other. For example, a library may wish to emphasize convenience for customers more than any of the other elements, and focus on improvements in that area. Another library may want to emphasize responsiveness. Both of these are significant aspects of customer service, but the point is that the library gets to choose which is more important to its particular situation.

By using a portable camcorder, librarians can collect information about cleanliness in the building and order on the shelves. Staff interactions with customers might be videotaped, preferably with a wall-mounted camera. The camera need not operate all the time. However, it should operate at random intervals, not just during the data collection periods. The idea is that staff should get so comfortable to the presence of the camera that they forget about it. Recording customer–staff interactions may cause some concern about the issue of privacy. Privacy, however, is a non-issue for several reasons, primarily because such interactions take place within sight and earshot of other people all the time. There is precedent; many organizations, including most financial services companies, utility companies, airline reservations, and the campus police, have used recordings of customer–staff interactions for a long time. A camera panning an automatic teller machine opposite the Alfred P. Murrah Federal Building supposedly recorded the rental truck used in the Oklahoma City bombing. The city of Baltimore's recent announcement that cameras would be installed on utility poles in high crime areas is another example of the increasing use of the cameras.

Videotape offers several advantages over simple observation. It provides a record that can be used to show comparisons in situations over time. Video also allows many people to view a situation, resulting in greater agreement about what has been seen on the tape. Lastly, it is useful in disputes: if, for example, a particular section of shelving usually seems in disarray, and the section is filmed, it becomes difficult to dispute the fact of disarray. Videotape can also be used to document lapses in building maintenance to those in charge of campuswide facilities.

BEHAVIORAL OBSERVATIONS

Our considerations concerning customer–staff interactions are based on observed behaviors. Much has been written on the behaviors desired of library staff, especially of reference staff (e.g., Larson & Dickson, 1994; Layman & Vandercook, 1990). Based on that literature, some conclusions about the quality of service can be drawn. Customers do not always know if the service is good or bad; they just know how they feel about it.

Table 6.1 presents methods to be used to collect the data elements related to the Service Quality Information Checklist (SQIC). The symbols at the beginning relate to the different data collection methods, indicating how information about particular aspects of service might be collected. It merits noting that some data elements have intentionally been given two symbols; redundant measures allow a view of the same thing in a different way.

Table 6.1. Service Quality Checklist

+ = service that can be answered by a yes or no
S = service that can be monitored by sampling/observation (preferably by videotape)
P = service that can be monitored by telephone records
O = service that can be monitored by OPAC
T = service that can be monitored by response time
C = service that can be monitored by customer response
N = service that can be monitored by a count of items
L = service that can be monitored by a listing of items

Resources: Information Content

(C) Appropriateness of fit (match) between content and customer
(T) The library quickly updates catalog records for lost items
(O) Recent books and journals are available
(T) Shelving of new materials in relation to publication date
(C) Information pertinent to customer requests is available

The Organization: Its Service Environment and Resource Delivery

---

Convenience
    (+ and P) OPAC can be accessed via modem
    (N and L) OPAC provides gateways to journal indexes and other library catalogs
    (+) Can renew items via OPAC or by some other electronic means
    (+) Can recall items via OPAC or some other electronic means
    (+ and N) OPAC terminals are available throughout the library
    (+ and T) Wait for service at public service points is not more than a few minutes
    (+) Library service policies are available online
    (+) Reference questions can be posed and answered online
    (+) Reference sources such as dictionaries and encyclopedia can be accessed via modem
    (+ and N) CD-ROMs can be accessed via modem
    (+) User guides available online
Hours of operation
    (+) Available by phone or online
    (+) Are posted on door
    (+) Information is printed on bookmark for later reference
    (+) Information is updated to accommodate holidays, including on bookmark
    (+ and N) Open evenings and weekends
    (+) "Special units" are open hours other than 9 a.m. to 5 p.m.
Location (e.g., of library or collection)
    (+) Available parking is nearby (i e, would you be willing to walk this distance to use the library? (If lot is always full, parking is unavailable)
    (+) Drive up book drop is available
Efficiency
    (+ and z) Items are quickly reshelved
    (+ and S) Materials are in correct order on the shelves
    (+ and T) Interlibrary loans are processed quickly
    (+ and T) Same day notification given for arriving interlibrary loans
    (+ and T) Items for reserve are processed quickly
    (+ and T) Serials are bound promptly at the end of the volume year

Staffing (service time and availability—queuing)
- (+)   Staff wear some identification so they can be easily identified
- (+)   Service points have sufficient staff to accommodate customers
- (+)   Staff is available throughout building to help customers and not all concentrated in traditional public service areas.

Public service departments are open when building is
- (+)   open on weekends
- (+ and N) open evenings

Equipment—in operating condition
- (S)   Percentage of OPAC terminals working
- (S)   Percentage of OPAC terminals in use
- (+)   Printouts possible (i e. working printer with paper)
- (S)   Percentage of CD-ROMS working
- (S)   Percentage of CD-ROMs in use
- (+)   Printouts possible
- (S)   Percentage of copy machines working
- (S)   Percentage of copy machines in use
- (+)   Copy machines accept both coins and cards
- (+)   Instructions for cards are clear and visible
- (+)   Instructions for recharging photocopy cards are clear and visible
- (S)   Percentage of microform readers working
- (S)   Percentage in use
- (+)   Operating instructions clearly posted
- (+)   Directions for retrieving films and fiche posted
- (+)   Instructions are clear and visible for reporting malfunctions or broken equipment
- (+)   Broken equipment removed or clearly marked
- (+)   Pencil sharpeners available and notice of their availability visible

Equipment not available, awaiting repair
- (N)   Photocopiers
- (N)   Terminals
- (N)   Microform readers

Responsiveness, Including Complaint and Compliment Procedures

Follow-through procedures are standard
- (+ and T) Customers requesting purchase of a title are notified promptly as to outcome and arrival
- (+ and T) Faculty are notified when materials requested for reserve room are available or not available

Ease of making complaint or compliment
- (+)   It is clear where to go to with a problem

Complaint may be made
- (+ and N) by phone
- (+ and N) in person
- (+ and N) by e-mail
- (+ and N) by letter
- (+)   Staff member is there to take complaint
- (C or S) Staff member seems interested in the problem
- (C or S) Staff member appears to believe the customer

Response/redress for receiving poor service
- (C or S) Does the staff member solve or try to solve the problem?
- (C or S) If not, does the staff member indicate that the problem will be investigated?

(C or S) If so, is the customer told that the library will try to solve the problem and the approximate length of time it will take?

(C or S) If so, will the customer be notified of the disposition of the problem?

(C) Does the customer feel satisfied at the conclusion of the interaction with the staff member?

(+) If the customer wants to see an administrator, is one available?

(C or S) Are complaints handled with courtesy and empathy, or are the customers considered bothersome?

(C or S) Does staff try to "justify" the library in handling the complaint?

(C) Does the customer feel satisfied at the end?

(+) Does the staff ask if the customer is satisfied with the way the complaint was handled?

Physical Surroundings

Ambient conditions
(C and S) Noise level is low
(S) Building is clean
(+) Restrooms are available
(S) Restrooms are clean
(S) Shelves are in order
(S) Piles of books are not lying around
(S) Furniture is not broken or torn
(+) Places for quiet study are available
(+) Personal safety/security is high
(N) Number of incidents of theft, assault or molestation in past 12 months

Spatial Layout & Signage
(+) Directory and floor plan visible on entering the building
(+) Signs pointing to catalog, reference, loan, etc.
(+) Prominently displayed signs on each floor indicating call number locations
(+) Information on OPAC also shows location of item if "in library," not just call number

Service Costs

(N) Photocopy page charges
(N) ILL charges
(N) Overdue charges

Service Reputation (e. g., as service-oriented)

Customer regularly returns...would return only in dire emergency
(C) to particular staff member
(C) to particular department
(C and O) to library
(C) Customer tells friends about library experiences

Service Delivery: Staff

Public Service Staff
(S) Willing to give instructions on using OPACs, etc.
(+) Knowledgeable staff (not just students) on duty

Behavior
- (S and C) Approachable/welcoming
- (S and C) Appropriate body language and a smile
- (S and C) Courteous
- (C) Empathetic
- (S and C) Staff is responsive to customer request/transaction
- (S and C) Friendly/pleasant
- (S and C) Includes user in search process (i. e not ignoring customer's presence)
- (S) Maintains eye contact
- (S) Willing to leave the desk to assist customer
- (C) Ability to determine what customers need

Systems/Technical Service Staff
  Service orientation
- (+) Considers/welcomes customer recommendations
  Speed of delivery (e.g., in order & processing)
- (T) Receipt of new materials in relation to publication date
- (O) Cataloging and processing of materials
- (N) Number of items in the backlog

Speed of Delivery (Mechanical and Human)

- (+ and T) Most questions are answered the same day
- (C) Sufficient amount of assistance provided, including the amount of time needed to respond to a request
- (S and C) Staff goes with customer to shelf to identify items
- (S and C) Staff follows through to check if customer is satisfied
- (S and C) If person on duty can't answer question, goes to find someone who can

THE CYCLE OF DATA COLLECTION

A common argument against data collection is that it takes too much staff time and effort. That argument is not valid in the SQIS. Many items reflective of service quality can be checked once, unless circumstances change. Much of the representative data can be gathered automatically via such computerized systems as the OPAC. Cyclic data elements need be sampled on a schedule to be determined by the library. For those areas that seem to be working well during an evaluation period, there is no need for constant monitoring. However, areas where service requires major improvement need more frequent monitoring. Response time data should be gathered on a regular schedule, the numbers entered onto a computer spreadsheet program and evaluated at regular intervals. Unit supervisors should keep cyclic and response time trend data to compare changes over time. Table 6.2 shows the data collection periods for the different service quality elements.

Table 6.2. Service Quality Information System Data Collection Cycle

Non-Recurring Data Collection

Information about the following service elements needs to be gathered just once, unless circumstances change. However, review these items periodically, just to make sure that nothing has changed.

Hours of operation
- Available by phone or online
- Posted on door
- Information is printed on bookmark for later reference
- Open evenings and weekends
- "Special units" are open hours other than just 9 a.m. to 5 p.m.
- All public service departments are open when building is open on weekends

Staff
- Staff wear some identification, perhaps name tags, so they can be easily identified
- Students do not work alone in public service departments

Equipment
- Are instructions as to how to report malfunctions or broken equipment clearly visible in all areas containing equipment

  Photocopy machines
  - Do copy machines accept coins as well as cards?
  - Are the instructions for cards clear and visible?
  - Are the instructions for recharging photocopy cards clear and visible?
  Microfilm/Microfiche readers
  - Are operating instructions clearly posted?
  - Are directions for retrieving films and fiche posted?
  Pencil sharpeners
  - Are available
  - Is notice of their location visible?

Building layout
- Directory and floor plan visible on entering the building
- Signs pointing to catalog, reference, loan, etc.
- Signs on each floor indicating call number locations
- Information on OPAC also shows location of item if "in library"
- Restrooms are available

Cyclical Data Collection

The information about the service elements listed below should be gathered on a recurring basis and the newest data compared with the previous data on a trend line.

Equipment—These data should be recorded on the form provided in Chapter 7.
  Terminals
  - Percentage of terminals working
  - Percentage of terminals in use
  - Are printouts possible (i.e. working printer with paper)?

CD-ROM units
  • Percentage of CD-ROMs working
  • Percentage of CD-ROMs in use
Photocopy machines
  • Percentage of photocopy machines working
  • Percentage of photocopy machines in use
Microform readers
  • Percentage of readers working
  • Percentage of readers in use
  • Are printouts possible?
  • Is broken equipment removed or clearly marked?

Physical Surroundings (Suggest the use of a portable camcorder for these)
  • Building is clean
  • Restrooms are clean
  • Shelves are in order
  • Piles of books are not lying around
  • Furniture is not broken or torn

Staff (Again, use of a wall-mounted camcorder will be helpful for these data elements)
  • Service points have sufficient staff to accommodate customers
  • Staff is welcoming
  • Staff is responsive to customer request/transaction
  • Staff is knowledgeable in responding to request/not just students on duty
  • Staff goes with customer to shelf to identify items
  • Staff follows through to check if customer is satisfied
  • Staff is available throughout building to help customers and not all concentrated in traditional public service areas
  • If student on duty cannot answer question, goes to find someone who can
  • Staff willing to give instructions on OPACs, etc.

Customers:
  • Number of customers waiting at service points such as circulation and reference
  • Customer focus groups
  • Follow up on complaints to see if customers are satisfied
  • Number of reports to campus police involving customer safety or property
  • Numbers and type of complaints not involving police reports

Response Times

Collection of data about the following should be based on the average time for each of the service elements.

  • *Processing materials*—Average number of days from arrival of new material until available for checkout.
  • *Reshelving materials*—Average number of days from return until in proper place on shelves.
  • *Processing interlibrary loan*—Average number of days from customer request to request sent to lending library.
  • *Customers notified of arrival of ILL*—Average number of days from arrival of borrowed material until customer is notified.
  • *Processing items for reserve after receipt*—Average number days from receipt of

reserve list from faculty until materials are ready for student checkout. These data are collected only for the first month of each semester and the first week of summer terms.

- *Equipment is not available because it is awaiting repair*—Average number of days for repair of equipment.
- *Serials unavailable because of binding*—Average number of days from removing serials from public areas until the bound volumes are reshelved.
- *Complaint responses*—Average response time to respond to complaints.
- *Complaint corrections*—Average response time to redress/fix complaints.

CONSIDERING INTANGIBLES IN SERVICE QUALITY

"Library service lies somewhere between" stores offering products and service agencies offering physical goods as well as service, said Emery (1993). He considered printed works (now also electronic data) as products having intangible benefits attached to them. These benefits include reducing mental discomfort arising from a consciousness of ignorance, boredom, or a lack or self-fulfillment (p. 16). He also defined benefits in terms of recreation, information, economic advantage, or self-improvement. In return for goods and services received, customers spend time or money (either as user fees or through their local taxes).

Because service products are intangible:

> The way customers judge a service may depend as much or even more on the service process than on the service outcome...the how of service delivery is a key part of the service....Purchasers of services judge quality on the basis of experiences they have during the service process as well as what might occur afterwards. (Berry, Bennett, & Brown, 1989, p. 34)

We agree with Berry et al., but we also considered factors important to users of any service. These include convenience; cost in terms of time, money, and annoyance; responsiveness of both the service operation itself and the staff; and customer expectations. Reliability is another factor considered; can users depend on information obtained from library staff, from catalog records, and from library resources? Staff competence also influences service quality. Competence can also include response time—the length of time that it takes to catalog and process items, for instance, indicates the competence of the technical services units.

Some of these measures reflect dimensions also noted in SERVQUAL, service measures widely known in the marketing literature (see Chapter 3 and Parasuraman, Zeithaml, & Berry, 1988). Texas A&M University has developed a model having five dimensions of service quality called RATER. RATER's dimensions, which are essentially identical to those in SERVQUAL, include ("Keeping the Customer Satisfied," 1994, p. 10):

- Reliability. The ability to provide what was promised. This dimension includes dependability and accuracy.
- Assurance. The knowledge and courtesy of employees and their ability to convey trust and confidence.
- Tangibles. The physical facilities and its equipment.
- Empathy. The care and attention provided to customers.
- Responsiveness. The willingness to help and provide prompt service.

Some items from the SQIS are regrouped in Table 6.3 to show how they reflect the dimensions of both SERVQUAL and RATER.[1]

Table 6.3. Elements of SERVQUAL/RATER in Relationship to Service Quality Information System

SERVQUAL/RATER Elements	Service Quality Measures
Reliability	Resources: 　Accuracy 　Comprehensiveness 　Relevance to request Staff: 　Accuracy in answering questions 　Follows through to ensure that customer is 　　satisfied
Assurance	Staff: 　Approachable/courteous 　Able to negotiate the library system and 　　records to help customers 　Knowledgeable about user needs 　Knowledge of information issues 　Technical expertise (formats, Internet) 　Willing to help 　Able to communicate with staff in other units
Tangibles	Equipment: 　In operating condition 　Provides options such as coin/card 　Operating instructions are clear Building: 　Clean 　Shelves are in order 　Furniture is not broken/torn 　Quiet places available 　Directory and floor plan at entry 　Signs prominently displayed on each floor to help

---

[1] Only the top five factors from SERVQUAL have been used in this section.

Empathy	Staff:
	Appropriate fit between content–customer
	Responsive to customer request
	Includes customer in search process
	Willing to leave the desk to help
	Quickly notifies customer about ILL arrivals and
	purchase requests
Responsiveness	Resources:
	New materials available
	Quick reshelving of items
	Organization:
	Convenience
	Dial access to OPAC
	Can renew online
	Hours of operation
	Location of parking
	Book drop
	All departments open evenings and weekends
	Staff:
	Easy to identify
	Sufficient staff to help
	Complaints:
	Ease of making complaint
	Quick response/redress

COLLECTIONS AND CUSTOMERS

Academic libraries have traditionally focused attention on collections—and most particularly on building bigger ones—based on the premise that the greater the number of items, the better the library; ergo, quantity of volumes equals quality of service. (The idea of bigger equals better has, of course, come under question by the woes of such corporate giants as General Motors and IBM.) To keep up with the quantity of materials being published, libraries have turned over much of the responsibility for materials selection to vendors who match select titles to profiles developed by the libraries.

However, academic librarians have not seriously analyzed how customers actually use their collections, nor have they expressed much interest in learning about customer frustrations in coping with items that are missing or are wanted but not purchased. In short, most library administrators have not studied how their collections satisfy customers or incorporated those kinds of data in acquisitions decisions. The opportunity to analyze collection use, however, has arrived with the installation of OPACs.

The new technologies offer a great opportunity to enhance service quality and customer satisfaction. Many OPACs give a good, though incomplete, picture of how the collection is being used and, to some degree, whether it meets customer expectations. Here are some of the elements built into to many OPACs that could be highly useful in understanding customer needs and how well the collection satisfies them. OPACs can tally searches by author, title, and subject (name or keyword). The systems can also tally the relationship between hits and misses for each category. From these data it is possible to calculate:

- The percentage of items searched for that are owned by the library;
- The percentage listed as "in library" and the percentage that are "on loan;"
- Of those titles listed "in library," the percentage that were subsequently checked out, and the percentage that were not;
- Of those titles not checked out, the percentage that the customer did not find, including the number really missing;
- The types of items searched for in the OPAC that the library did not own;
- The types of items that have not been checked out in a long time; and
- Whether items not checked out for a long time are sitting on shelves or are missing.

OPACs can also track circulation by category of borrower: undergraduate, graduate, faculty, retired faculty, staff, and public. Many of these data can be cross-tabulated with each other on a spreadsheet program. Then a statistical package designed for microcomputers such as the *Statistical Package for the Social Sciences* (SPSS) can be used to test for significant relationships between such elements as hits for items owned searched by undergraduates.

It is possible to convert some of the data calculations into *outcome measures,* for example, the:

Ownership

$$\frac{\text{number of items searched for that the library system owns}}{\text{number of items searched for in the OPAC}} = \underline{\quad}\%$$

Availability

$$\frac{\text{number of items found}}{\text{number of items listed as "in library"}} = \underline{\quad}\%$$

Both of these examples center on the OPAC. The first measure recognizes that OPACs list holdings for more than one library (within and across systems), whereas the second measure can be converted into an indication of the number of titles on the shelf in proper location as opposed to those mis-shelved, waiting reshelving, or left on tables.

BENCHMARKING

Many academic libraries are now conducting benchmarking or are considering doing so. Benchmarking is a systematic analysis (including time and motions expended) of the way that a particular task is performed. An example of such a process is the movement of new books through cataloging and processing to reach the shelves. Benchmarking can be used for several purposes. One is for comparison with the "best in class." Many academic libraries are interested in benchmarking to compare their results with those of peer libraries, just as they do with input statistics or measures. If this is the intent, and the marking occurs just once, or once every few years, it is not useful in terms of improving customer service. For example, what if the comparison reveals that, on average, serials prepared for binding are unavailable to customers for four months. Should this be considered acceptable service because the library's average matches well with its peers? Are the data outdated? How often should new data be produced?

A more important purpose of benchmarking is continuous improvement: to indicate how a situation has changed since it was last studied. For example, benchmarking can show materials are being reshelved more quickly (or more slowly) now than they were a year (or some other time period) ago. Using benchmarking to improve customer service requires periodic monitoring, not just taking an occasional snapshot.

Benchmarking has one drawback: "Quality improvement programs tend to enhance existing processes rather than aim for breakthrough changes that will replace old processes with new" (Shapiro & Long, 1994, p. 286). However, even incremental improvements can enhance customer service if benchmarking is approached from that perspective.

The value of benchmarking is not as a vehicle for making comparisons among libraries, but rather as a way for a library to monitor its own performance. Benchmarking can also assist administrators in understanding better processes and policies and use the insights gained in conjunction with feedback from customers and employees. The purpose is to establish unit goals and objectives that are in line with customer expectations.

PROGRESS THROUGH PROCESS

"How the work gets done in an organization should be driven by end user requirements" (Seymour, 1995, p. 23). If response times seem overlong for a particular task, the reasons for delay can frequently be uncovered by study-ing the process used to complete the task. A *process* is a series of activities, done in a certain order, to accomplish a task. For example, the steps involved in checking out an item by the circulation department constitute a process. The totality of a library's service is an accretion of many processes, as mate-rials and information are handed off from one person to another, like a "relay team" (p. 53). Each hand-off should add value and be necessary to the fulfillment of the library's mission. When processes are not driven by cus-tomer needs, "the process...degrades into one that operates for the conve-nience of the people who work in the process, rather than for the customer of the service"(p. 23).

Academic libraries have tended to be organized according to functions (as depicted by the boxes in an organizational chart) with little consideration of processes. Function has been more important than process, and, as a result, fiefdoms strongly resistant to change have been allowed to dominate the ways in which work and services are performed. Many processes that are outmoded, slow, and cumbersome are continued just because that is the way things have always been done.

Two overriding principles should govern the analysis of process, "whether the goal is incremental improvement or radical innovation" (Seymour, 1995, p. 23). First, all process should be driven by customer requirements, not staff preferences or convenience. Second, manage-ment must develop appropriate measures to monitor processes so that outputs can be continually evaluated and improved. Process analysis allows managers to identify inefficiencies in the system caused by exces-sive use of time, materials, or energy. Surely a flawed process is to blame if it takes an average of 152.9 days to catalog a science book whose record can be found in the RLIN database (Page & Reagor, 1994). Such inefficiencies frequently and justifiably cause both employee and cus-tomer irritation.

Process analysis also identifies places or work points where demand exceeds the capacity of resources (either human or mechanical). It allows managers to monitor each step in a process to determine the value of its contribution to the entire library system and helps them determine places where the process breaks down because of lack of oversight. A com-mon breakdown is associated with the management of current periodicals in libraries lacking separate periodicals departments. Since no one is assigned to monitor performance or even provide customer service between the time that the issues are checked in as received until they are gathered for binding or replaced by microform copy, it is no wonder such departments may be chaotic. Best of all, processes analysis uncovers activities that need not be done at all, such as (in some instances) pasting in book pockets.

INFORMATION, NOT DATA, PLEASE

A library director on the panel at the AMIGOS meeting (see Chapter 4) commented that her problem was not lack of data, but rather so much data that she did not know how to process it. Her perspective was most helpful because it serves as a reminder that top administrators need information, not undigested data. Deans and directors need different kinds of information for different purposes. For budgets they need cost and spending information; for staffing they require productivity data. The information system presented here deals only with elements of service quality which have been identified as important by librarians in our focus groups and customers responding to our questionnaires (see Chapter 4). Furthermore, the data have been distilled for administrators to convey information useful in pinpointing areas for improving customer service.

Unit managers need a great deal of data about their units, but chief administrators require only information about the things important to customer service and the library's mission. What follows in Table 6.4 are the elements from each unit that the chief administrators should ponder.

Table 6.4. Top Administrators' Data Requirements

Information from the OPAC

- The relationship of hits to misses in author, title, and subject searches.
- The percentage of circulation for each major classification in relation to the percentage of the collection represented by that class. Suppose the BF section (psychology) represents 2% of the collection, yet accounts for 4.7% of the circulation. This information allows the comparison of acquisitions in a classification section with the relative use of the section, and may suggest a change in acquisition policy.
- If dial-up OPAC access is offered, the ratio of searches by modem to total OPAC searches might be compared.
- The percentage of searches for items in circulation compared to the percentage listed as "in library."
- The number of titles in each classification section that have not circulated since a given date. It is even more helpful if the data can be subdivided by date of publication of the non-circulated titles.

Information from the Systems Unit

- Downtime of the OPAC system because of malfunction or system work.
- Total downtime of individual OPAC terminals.
- Downtime of the library's local area network (LAN).

Information from the Access Services Department

- The average time to reshelve materials used in the library.
- The average time to reshelve circulated materials.
- Total in-library circulation as estimated from barcode scanning.
- Total checked-out circulations.

Information from Technical Services Units

- Number of items in the cataloging backlog/frontlog, and the percentage increase or decrease from the previous reporting period.
- Average number of days between receipt of new materials and the time they are placed on the shelves. If type of material (e.g., foreign-language items) is a factor, the information should be broken down by the significant categories.
- Average number of days for check-in of new issues of serials.
- Average number of days that serials are unavailable because of binding.

Information from Public Service Units

- Proportion of phone callers to receiving busy signals.
- Downtime of terminals and related equipment.
- Summary report on staff knowledge and behaviors from groups viewing videotapes.

Information from Each Library Unit (Branches, Departments, and Teams)

- Specific customer complaints. These should include informal complaints made to staff, such as complaints about long lines for service or missing materials.
- Specific action taken on each complaint.
- Suggestions as to how to improve service.

Responsibility for data collection should rest with the units concerned with the work being analyzed. The units should not only monitor themselves, but also be responsible for initiating improvements to enhance customer satisfaction (e.g., faster response times and better anticipation of customer needs). The units' reports should focus on improvement until an optimum situation is achieved. The next chapter presents specific instructions and forms for units to collect data on some aspects of service quality.

CONCLUSION

The SQIS is intended to assist libraries to identify data pertinent to customer needs and to better manage that information in order to streamline service. However, the information collected is inert; only people can translate information into action—action that will enhance service quality for all of the library's customers.

Chapter 7

Looking at
Service Quality
in Your Library

Left to our own devices, we pay too much attention to things of too little importance to the customer.

—Seymour, 1995, p. 14

Quality is everyone's job. But it's management's responsibility.

—Guaspari, 1985, p. 65

B arriers that hinder customers from getting what they want, and the frustration resulting from useless or wasted effort or failure to understand the intricacies of how the library is organized, strongly influence customer perceptions of service quality. As a result, improvements in quality must remove or lower those barriers and frustrations. This chapter's illustrative discussion and tables should assist librarians in collecting data about barriers and other factors likely to cause or heighten customer frustration. These data reflect some, but not all, elements of library service that are important to customers; for this reason, libraries should consider the adoption of an automated complaint management system. The data are useful to library administrators, but even more so to unit managers and their staffs, in helping them to evaluate whether certain activities need revision, monitoring, or major change.

The data gathered from using the techniques presented in this chapter are not adequate for all administrative needs relating to service quality. The examples and tables are illustrative rather than comprehensive, and the techniques are confined to factors identified by focus groups and by customer responses to the two questionnaires as important (See Chapter 4). Furthermore, data collection is relatively easy to do and to monitor.

This chapter covers:

- Responsibility for collecting the data;
- What data should be collected and how;
- The forms for recording and reporting the data;
- Sharing the data/information with other units;
- Analyzing the data; and
- Building a information system for the library administration.

WHO SHOULD COLLECT DATA ON SERVICE QUALITY?

The unit responsible for the service should collect the data, whether a department, a team, or a sub-unit. Assigning the people responsible for the service to collect data about their contributions gives them a personal stake in its quality. This also gives the unit staff responsibility for ensuring the reliability, validity, and acceptability of the data. Nonetheless, managers should take precautions to ensure data integrity.

The data should be reported to the unit manager/team leader for aggregation, but not simply to be forwarded to the library's administration. It is crucial that the manager share the data with all members of the unit to give everyone a sense of responsibility for the results and their integrity. Results in this context encompass much more than merely the number of units of work processed; they should focus on speed, quality, and responsiveness. As part of the sharing process, the manager should lead staff members in a discussion on what, if anything, they intend to do about the quality of service in their section and specific plans for change. The sharing and discussion of unit data result in heightened awareness of everyone's responsibility for the quality of the service delivered by each unit and the value of striving to meet the organization's mission and vision.

Assigning data collection responsibility to units will probably reveal elements of importance to customers for which no library unit is responsible. For example, many libraries allow outside vendors to install photocopiers. The library disclaims any responsibility for the operation or, more likely, non-operation of the machines. Building maintenance is another area in which library staff might not be responsible for oversight. If a central campus unit services all buildings, then who in the library monitors maintenance beyond the purview of that unit (e.g., the condition of the furniture or decisions about where signs are needed)?

Some elements of customer service are based on decisions made by the administration—whether staff wear some kind of identification or whether information about library hours is available by a recorded phone message. Since these decisions are infrequently changed, the administrator responsible for the decision should indicate the policy. The purpose is to have each administrator think about the policy in terms of its contribution to service quality.

WHAT DATA SHOULD BE COLLECTED AND HOW

The service quality information system should only include data reflective of customer service. These include turnaround times, the reliability of equipment (from photocopiers to local area networks), convenience for internal and external customers, ease of use of the facility, ambient conditions such as acceptable temperature and noise levels, and the assurance of security for persons and property.

Some elements of service quality, such as signage indicating the various service areas in the library, are not readily changed. Other elements require regular monitoring to assess whether service quality is changing, especially in the direction that the unit wants to go. Another reason for regular monitoring is to keep staff focused on the importance of service quality. Some specific examples of services which need regular monitoring include:

- Reshelving times for returned items;
- Processing times for new materials;
- The condition of equipment for customer use; and
- Turnaround times for interlibrary loans (both borrowing and lending).

The library administration and the units involved, after establishing a baseline number, should decide how frequently these activities are monitored. However, the unit manager responsible, all the unit staff, and every senior administrator should know the response times for the items listed above. If they do not, they have little knowledge of the quality of service that customers receive.

Many of the service quality elements can be answered with a yes or no: either the library does or does not offer a particular service, or it has or lacks a particular policy. Table 7.1 provides a mechanism for analyzing administrative decisions about service or policy. This table simply calls for a yes or no response. While most of the yes or no factors are static, circumstances sometimes cause changes. For example, hours of operation may change because of increases or decreases in library funding, or, more commonly, because of the shift to or from summer or vacation hours. It is a good idea to take stock of the yes/no elements at least every six months and note changed conditions. Others can be answered by a number which may change as new services, such as more gateways to other databases or equipment, are added.

Table 7.1. Policies Affecting Service Quality

Answer the following with YES /NO

OPAC

OPAC can be accessed via modem
OPAC provides gateways to journal indexes
OPAC provides gateways to other library catalogs
Can recall/reserve items via the OPAC
Can flag items to be placed in reserve room via OPAC
OPAC terminals are available throughout the library
Assistance provided for electronic services (e.g., help screens, online tutorials, and publicized help phone for assistance)
OPAC shows last issue received for journals

Electronic Media Are Easily Available

Library service policies are available online
Reference questions can be posed and answered online
Reference sources such as dictionaries and encyclopedia can be accessed via modem
CD-ROMs can be accessed via modem
User guides available online

Hours of Operation

Available by phone or by net
Information is printed on bookmark for later reference
Information is updated to accommodate holidays, including on bookmark
Open evenings
Open weekends
"Special Units" are open evenings
"Special Units" are open weekends

Location (e.g., of library or collection)

Available parking is nearby (You would be willing to walk this distance with an armload of books. Do not count parking areas which are always full.)
Drive up book drop is available

Staffing (service time and availability—queuing)

Staff members wear some identification, such as name tags so they can be easily identified
Service points have sufficient staff to accommodate customers
Staff is available throughout building to help customers and not all concentrated in traditional public service areas
Public service departments are open when building is open

Professional staff is available during evening hours
Knowledgeable staff, not just students on duty

Building Facilities

Restrooms are available
Drinking fountains available

Spatial Layout and Signage

Directory and floor plan visible on entering the building
Signs point to public catalog, reference, loan, etc.
Signs displayed on each floor indicate call number locations
Information on OPAC also shows call number and physical location (by floor number or
department) of items "in library"

Equipment

Instructions are clear and visible for reporting malfunctions or broken equipment.
Broken equipment removed or clearly marked
Pencil sharpeners
    available
    notice of their location visible
Photocopiers
    Machines accept coins as well as photocopy cards
    Instructions for photocopy cards are clear and visible
    Instructions for recharging photocopy cards are clear and visible
Microform Readers
    Operating instructions are clearly posted
    Directions for retrieving films and fiche posted

Responsiveness

Signs indicate where to go when customer has a problem
Customers requesting purchase of a title are notified on arrival/outcome
Faculty are notified when reserve materials are not available

---

After Table 7.1 has been completed, the senior administrative group
should study the responses in terms of how library policies and activities
facilitate or diminish service to customers. They should make adjustments
as necessary.

SHARING DATA WITH OTHER UNITS

The library is a system composed of parts that have to work together to opti-
mize service quality (See Chapter 2), and certain information about service
quality must be shared with other library units. Librarians responsible for

selecting materials need information from the library systems unit about authors, titles, and subjects searched for in the online public access catalog (OPAC) that were not purchased by the library. The intent is not to say that such materials should be ordered, but to study the data for patterns indicating areas of patron interest that might be incorporated into decisions about purchases. Selectors need information gathered from the circulation/access unit about the subjects or areas of the library classification having high and low circulation so that they can make better decisions about future selections and perhaps make adjustments to the approval plan profile. They also need information from the interlibrary loan (ILL) staff about the types of ILL requests to identify candidates for purchase.

Circulation/access staff need to know approximately how long it takes for materials ordered to arrive and be processed. This information enables them to give customers inquiring about the availability of new titles some indication of whether the waiting time exceeds their personal deadlines, or if the staff need to develop strategies for resolving or lessening bottlenecks. Data collected by the acquisitions, cataloging, and processing units should be shared with their internal customers, the circulation and information services units. Conversely, the circulation and information services units should be equally as forthcoming. Data sharing heightens the awareness of all units about the information needs, information preferences, and information-gathering behavior of both internal and external customers.

ANALYZING THE DATA

Data analysis which is the most difficult part of in-house evaluation involves shaping the data into coherent pieces for interpretation and action, as necessary. There are several ways to begin. One is to decide in advance on "acceptable" standards for service. An example is Federal Express' standard of seeking 100% service quality or perfect (problem-free) service to customers every day and subtracting mistakes from that score. Many libraries seem uncomfortable setting a standard for service since there are few instances of their doing that or of focusing on problems rather than presumed successes (e. g., the number of people served).

Another approach is to assess the status quo and decide if it is acceptable. Many libraries have assessed the status quo, but few have made decisions about the acceptability of the findings. An example is the oft-cited finding that reference staff are able to correctly answer about 55% of questions posed. A library can improve service quality by using either a priori standards or post priori data provided that it, so to speak, "keeps moving, to keep improving." However, if the library administration sets no standards for service such as turnaround times, then each employee decides his or her own work standards. Clearly, this sort of laissez-faire attitude is not customer-oriented.

Libraries should not monitor service quality once or twice a year, stuff the data in a file cabinet, and ignore the findings. The monitoring and improving of service quality have to be reinforced in the minds of all the staff so that they become guiding principles in doing their jobs. However, the customer has to be at the center of the service. Libraries exist only to serve customer information requests.

This section identifies some areas amenable to analysis and some strategies for improving service quality. It discusses the use of videotapes and data collection regarding response times (reshelving materials and serials), the extent to which customers encounter telephone busy signals, and downtimes. There is also discussion of the use of transaction logs.

Videotapes

Videotapes capture the state of building maintenance and disrepair, staff–customer interactions, and use of the building and its services. Not only do videos provide a historical and presumably impartial record which can be consulted as needed, they also allow different individuals to view the tapes for different purposes. One purpose is documentation of events or conditions. Another purpose is for groups to view the tapes to arrive at some consensus about whether what they see constitutes acceptable service quality in the library.

Staff–Customer Videos. Videotapes are a powerful tool for self-assessment. They can help staff members assess both their own behaviors and performance and that of the unit itself. The video interactions are not intended to be used for individual performance appraisals. The main purpose is for the unit to discuss what, if any, changes are needed by the unit as a unit.

Video cameras mounted in all reference areas in the library system, including all branches, could be activated at random intervals. Mounted cameras are less intrusive and less distracting to staff and customers, Videotapes of staff interacting with customers should be viewed by the staffs of the units involved. They should record their impressions on Table 7.2.

In large libraries, the tapes may record several staff–customer interactions going on at the same time. In that event, the machine should be stopped and the interaction to be recorded determined or, better yet, guidelines could be developed beforehand about how to handle such circumstances. The tapes can be replayed to capture information about the other interactions.

Some staff members may need help, either in knowledge of information resources or in interacting with customers. The unit manager at this point should play coach (the intent is not to penalize, but to assist the employee to meet service quality expectations). Berinstein (1995) offers a self-study program to assist reference staff to better understand the reference process and its relationship to customer satisfaction.

The tapes might also be viewed by an observer group composed of staff from the unit shown on the tape and other units, and customers. The intent is to get a sense of what is considered acceptable or unacceptable in terms of service quality. If more than one interaction appears on the tape, again, the group could select one or adhere to a set of guidelines.

The individuals in the groups should record their impressions on Table

Table 7.2. Customer—Staff Interaction: Individual Response

Unit Observed _____ Video number _____ Date of Taping _____

Please rate elements in the video showing customer-staff interaction on the basis of the items below. The rating scale is:

E = Excellent   S = Satisfactory   I = Improvement Needed   X = Does Not Apply

	E	S	I	X
Seems approachable				
Courteous				
Listens to customer				
Body language is open, relaxed				
Uses open questions to probe customer need				
Able to determine customer request				
Willing to leave desk if necessary				
Includes customer in search				
Expert in using electronic information or equipment, if necessary				
Demonstrates knowledge of appropriate information sources				
Provides material pertinent to customer request				
Appropriately refers customer to other agency or department				
Checks to ensure customer got needed information or materials				
Suggestions				

Group number_____Date_____

Table 7.3. Customer—Staff Interaction: Response from One Group

Unit Observed _____ Video number ____ Date of Taping _____
Number in Group_____ Group is: from unit____ Observer group ____

Tally the responses from individuals in the group and write the appropriate totals in each box. The rating scale is:

E = Excellent   S = Satisfactory   I = Improvement Needed   X = Does Not Apply

	E	S	I	X
Seems approachable				
Courteous				
Listens to customer				
Body language is open, relaxed				
Uses open questions to probe customer need				
Able to determine customer request				
Willing to leave desk if necessary				
Includes customer in search				
Expert in using electronic information or equipment, if necessary				
Demonstrates knowledge of appropriate information sources				
Provides material pertinent to customer request				
Appropriately refers customer to other agency or department				
Checks to ensure customer got needed information or materials				
TOTALS				

Group number_____Date_____

7.2 to allow for comparisons: (a) among members of the group, and (b) with the responses completed by the staff responsible for the service. These written impressions should enhance the development of a consensus about quality, rather than just the opinion of managers.

The manager of the information unit or branch should tally the responses from the observer group and share that information with the unit's staff. The point is to improve, not to penalize. Tables 7.3 and 7.4 offer examples of how to combine the data from the observer groups.

Table 7.3 summarizes one group's response, and Table 7.4 is a summary of responses from several groups.

Table 7.4. Customer—Staff Interaction:
Summary Report—Several Groups

Unit Observed _____ Video number _____ Date of Taping _____
Time period covered _____ Number of Groups_____

Tally the responses from the group reports and write the appropriate totals in each box. The rating scale is:

E = Excellent   S = Satisfactory   I = Improvement Needed   X = Does Not Apply

	E	S	I	X
Seems approachable				
Courteous				
Listens to customer				
Body language is open, relaxed				
Uses open questions to probe customer need				
Able to determine customer request				
Willing to leave desk if necessary				
Includes customer in search				
Expert in using electronic information or equipment, if necessary				
Demonstrates knowledge of appropriate information sources				
Provides material pertinent to customer request				
Appropriately refers customer to other agency or department				
Checks to ensure customer got needed information or materials				
TOTALS				

Group number_____Date_____

Videotapes can also help to uncover gaps between the collection and customers' information needs. For example, the tapes allow a record of unmet information requests to be created. These can be shared with selectors and factored into future acquisitions. The tapes also show activity levels in departments. For example, if there always seems to be a queue at reference/information service points, perhaps this will convince the administration that more staff is needed.

Building Maintenance.   The appearance of the building becomes readily apparent when taped. Periodically, someone should be designated to film shelving areas, study areas, restrooms, drinking fountains and other public spaces. Both the stack supervisor and the maintenance supervisor could use the tapes to monitor the work of their units. The employees involved could view the tapes, record their impressions on Table 7.5, and discuss what they saw in terms of acceptable service quality and what action, if any, should be taken as a result. Another observer group composed of staff from other units, customers and staff from the departments involved might review the tapes and note their reactions on Table 7.5. The responses of the observer group should be shared with staff from the units involved.

For illustrative purposes, Table 7.6 samples the responses from one group, and Table 7.7 summarizes responses from several groups over time.

Table 7.5.   Checklist for Physical Surroundings
Individual Response

Library Facility _____   Video # _____
                      (Name of Library)   Date of Taping _____

Use the following scale to rate your impressions of the condition of the library building as shown on the video

E = Excellent   S = Satisfactory   I = Improvement Needed   X = Does Not Apply

	E	S	I	X
Floor or Area examined				
Shelves in order				
Lighting is adequate				
Condition of furniture				
Cleanliness of public space				
Restrooms clean				
Drinking fountains clean				
Noise level acceptable				

Preparer:_____ Date:_____

Table 7.6. Checklist for Physical Surroundings
Group Response

Library Facility _____ Video # _____
(Name of Library)   Date of Taping _____
Number in Group _____

Tally the responses from the individual reports and write the appropriate totals in each box.

E = Excellent   S = Satisfactory   I = Improvement Needed   X = Does Not Apply

	E	S	I	X
Floor or Area examined				
Shelves in order				
Lighting is adequate				
Condition of furniture				
Cleanliness of public space				
Restrooms clean				
Drinking fountains clean				
Noise level acceptable				
TOTAL				

Preparer:_____ Date:_____

Table 7.7. Checklist for Physical Surroundings
Summary of Responses—Several Groups

Library Facility _____ Video # _____
(Name of Library)   Date of Taping _____
Number in Group _____   Time period covered _____

Tally the responses from all the group reports and write the appropriate totals in each box.

E = Excellent   S = Satisfactory   I = Improvement Needed   X = Does Not Apply

	E	S	I	X
Floor or Area examined				
Shelves in order				
Lighting is adequate				
Condition of furniture				
Cleanliness of public space				
Restrooms clean				
Drinking fountains clean				
Noise level acceptable				
TOTAL				

Preparer:_____ Date:_____

Response Times

Response times show how dedicated the library is to meeting customer needs. Some elements whose response time indicates service quality are:

- The availability of current monographs and serial issues;
- How quickly circulated items are reshelved;
- The wait for materials requested via interlibrary or intralibrary loan; and
- The ability to access the OPAC or library units by telephone.

Obviously high quality service prioritizes shortening customer waiting time as much as possible without diminishing quality. Judgments about appropriate response times should be based on the average time derived from the performance of everyone involved over several weeks, and a common sense standard of reasonableness. For example, Hébert (1994) found that some libraries did not even begin to process interlibrary loan requests for three weeks after the requests were submitted. In those cases, the average time exceeded any standard of reasonableness.

Reshelving Materials

Complaints about slow reshelving are common in many libraries. How quickly items that had been checked out are reshelved can be monitored by using colored slips of paper about the size of a bookmark. There should be a different color for each day of the week. As items are discharged, the slip is inserted so that it sticks out enough to be readily seen. Within a few days, simply by counting the slips by color it will be apparent how long items have been awaiting reshelving. The colored slips are also a reminder to the shelvers that their productivity is being monitored.

The slips can be inserted into materials used within the library either when their barcodes are wanded to count in-house circulation or by having someone insert them into materials lying on tables and book carts. Use Table 7.8 to record information for one week. Note that you must write in the colors selected for the slips each day. Obviously, the quicker the columns get to 0 the better the reshelving service.

Table 7.9 is a summary report for recording data from the weekly reports (Table 7.8). Table 7.9 reflects changes, if any, in the speed of the reshelving service.

Response Times for Serials. This refers to the time between arrival and initial shelving of current issues. It also includes the time between removal of issues for binding and their being reshelved. However, the availability of full text articles online reduces the number of issues received and volumes bound.

Telephone Calls

When customers calling the library for information about library hours, reference/information service or a connection to the library's online catalog encounter busy signals, they might become frustrated. As it is now possible to interact with the library's resources from one's home or office, more and more customers dial in for service, and expect to be connected. The library needs to know how many callers have received busy signals and on which lines, usually ones for the OPAC. This information can be obtained by contacting the local telephone company. Such information is helpful in documenting the need for more phone lines and in letting customers know the peak and slow times for phone access to the various units.

Table 7.8. Reshelving of Materials

Week of _____ Location _____
Write in the colors chosen for the slips for each day of the week
Mon_____ Tue_____ Wed_____ Thurs_____ Fri_____ Sat_____ Sun_____

Below indicate the number of slips of each color remaining on the shelves from previuous days.
Begin inserting slips on Monday and begin counting the related colored slips on Tuesday.

Day of count	Number of slips of a day's color found						
Monday		Tuesday Slips	Wednesday Slips	Thursday Slips	Friday Slips	Saturday Slips	Sunday Slips
Tuesday	Monday Slips		Wednesday Slips	Thursday Slips	Friday Slips	Saturday Slips	Sunday Slips
Wednesday	Monday Slips	Tuesday Slips		Thursday Slips	Friday Slips	Saturday Slips	Sunday Slips
Thursday	Monday Slips	Tuesday Slips	Wednesday Slips		Friday Slips	Saturday Slips	Sunday Slips
Friday	Monday Slips	Tuesday Slips	Wednesday Slips	Thursday Slips		Saturday Slips	Sunday Slips
Saturday	Monday Slips	Tuesday Slips	Wednesday Slips	Thursday Slips	Friday Slips		Sunday Slips
Sunday	Monday Slips	Tuesday Slips	Wednesday Slips	Thursday Slips	Friday Slips	Saturday Slips	

Table 7.9. Reshelving Summary Report

Time Period _____ Library or Branch _____

Tally the numbers from a group of Table 7.8 forms and record the number of volumes waiting to be shelved in the Number of days section below. The summary can include observations from a number of weeks or from a number of different locations. Note which in the left column.

Number of Volumes Not Reshelved

Location or date	Number of days unshelved									
	2	3	4	5	6	7	8	9	10	>10

Table 7.10 provides information related to telephone service. The completion of the table could be assigned to support staff. The issue is less who collects the data than that someone does so on a periodic basis.

Table 7.10. Availability of Telephone Access

Time Period Covered: _____

OPAC Calls

	Number of phone calls to library OPAC
	Number of calls to OPAC receiving busy signal
	Percentage of phone calls to OPAC receiving busy signal

Reference/Information Calls

	Number of phone calls to reference/information departments
	Number of calls to reference/information departments receiving busy signal
	Percentage of phone calls to reference/information departments receiving busy signal

Public Service Calls

	Number of phone calls to public service number
	Number receiving busy signal
	Percentage receiving busy signal

Name of Preparer: _____ Date: _____

Downtimes

Downtimes are another variant of response times, but are sufficiently significant that they should be separately reported. Downtimes refer to the number of minutes, hours, or days that equipment is inoperable for whatever reason. Equipment would include the OPAC system and any of its relevant modules (e.g., serials check-in). These can be monitored by using Table 7.11.

Downtimes should also be tracked for terminals serving the local area network, stand-alone terminals for CD-ROMs and all terminals linked to the OPAC. Equipment such as photocopiers and microform readers should also be included in downtime reports.

Table 7.11. Monthly OPAC Status Report

Date	/ /	/ /	/ /	/ /	/ /	/ /	/ /	/ /
Minutes entire system down								
Minutes sub-systems down								
Acquisitions								
Serials								
Cataloging								
Circulation								
Modem access								
Gateway 1								
Gateway 2								
Gateway 3								
Gateway 4								

Someone needs to check on the equipment at least once every day—including weekends. That means that the units responsible for the machines send staff members to assess their operating condition. Information about photocopiers, OPAC terminals and CD-ROM players can be collected by using Tables 7.12 through 7.14. Daily information should be cumulated weekly, monthly, and quarterly. The same table can be used for this purpose by noting the appropriate time period in the section marked "date."

These data are not simply to be filed and forgotten. The purpose of cumulation is to chart trends. Are certain machines always breaking, and if so, can they be replaced? Is there usually a queue waiting to use the machine, which would indicate a need for additional machines. If the library has a contract with an outside photocopy service, the data should be used at contract renewal time.

Backlogs, a corollary of response times, are the number of items awaiting whatever needs to be done to them in a particular unit. Backlogs are caused by understaffing, cumbersome and overly complicated workflow procedures, inattention to customer needs, special problems (e.g., cumulation of extensive holdings of foreign language publications requiring original cataloging), and poor planning—receipt of too many items at once.

(In some places the backlogs are so huge that the staff created another category called frontlog which contains the items from the backlog needing priority handling.) Whatever the reasons, eliminating backlogs should be a prime objective in enhancing service quality. It may turn out that the work causing the backlog does not need to be done at all.

Transaction Logs

Every OPAC system has its own advantages and limitations. It is not our attempt to discuss any one system here. All of them can generate helpful of reports provided that the systems staff set the parameters to produce them. (See Dynix, n.d. and CARL, 1994 as examples.) One feature that online public access catalogs can provide is a chronological list of searches conducted by users at terminals, these searches are known as transaction logs. Such logs are "the print product of the process whereby a system has been programmed to store on tape all of the activity occurring at a specified terminal connected to that system" (Wallace, 1993, p. 240); users are unaware that their searches are being recorded. The information obtained from the logs includes the date and time of each search along with the type of search and whether or not the search produced any hits, that is, bibliographic citations for the authors, titles or subjects/words searched.

There have been a number of studies of transaction logs, many of which have attempted to understand the search process or how humans formulate

Table 7.12. OPAC Terminals Status Report

	Location 1	Location 2	Location 3	Location 4	Location 5	Location 6		
Name								
Time:								
Date:								
# OPAC terminals								
# In use								
# Working/unoccupied								
# Not working								
# People waiting								
# Printers								
# Printers not working								
Comments								

Table 7.13. CD-ROM Status Report

	Location 1	Location 2	Location 3	Location 4	Location 5	Location 6
Name						
Time:						
Date:						
# CD-ROM terminals						
# In use						
# Working/unoccupied						
# Not working						
# People waiting						
# Printers						
# Printers not working						
Comments						

Table 7.14. Photocopiers Status Report

Name						
Time:						
Date:						
	Location 1	Location 2	Location 3	Location 4	Location 5	Location 6
# Photocopiers						
# In use						
# Working/unoccupied						
# Not working						
# People waiting						
Comments						

queries. Our interest here is to demonstrate on a macro level how the OPAC is being used, the relationship between hits and searches, and the reasons for search failure—there was no hit.

By using Table 7.15, the system staff can monitor the types of searches done on the OPAC. Any terminals primarily used by library staff, should be excluded because the intent is to study how customers fared in their searches. Table 7.16 examines the reasons why customers failed to find any materials related to their searches.

The library administration will determine how often transaction logs are analyzed and how many (and which) terminals are involved. However, the library might experiment with the use of transaction log analysis in order to obtain some understanding of how users interact with the OPAC remotely and internal to the library (see Lucas, 1993). This knowledge should indicate the extent to which further analysis of the logs is necessary.

Table 7.15. Transaction Log
OPAC Searches by Type and Hit Rate

Library _____ Terminal(s) _____ Date(s) _____

T=Title
A/N=Author or Name
S=Subject
K/W=Keyword or Word
B=Boolean (any combination of name or subject)
C=Call Number
O=Other

Search Type	Searches with hits	Zero-hit searches	Zero hits as % of type	Type of search as % of total
T				
A/N				
S				
K/W				
B				
C				
O				
TOTAL				

Library _____ Date(s) _____

**Table 7.16. Transaction Log
Problem Analysis**

Library _____ Terminal(s) _____ Date(s) _____

Type of Error	Type of Search						Total	
	T	A/N	S	K/W	B	C	Number	Percent
Typo								
Spelling								
Not owned								
Reversed Name								
Format not in OPAC								
Other								
Total								

Library _____ Date(s) _____

Determining success or failure in using an OPAC is an extremely complicated subject which is influenced by the users' previous experience with the system, the words chosen for the search and their match with the capabilities of the system, and a number of other factors such as too many titles retrieved and false drops. However, two basic factors in customer satisfaction in using the OPAC are getting: (a) on a terminal and (b) a hit for the search tried. Customers errors frequently result in not getting a hit. These errors include typographical errors, misspellings, not putting last name first in systems having that requirement and looking for material not covered by the OPAC (See Peters, 1989, p. 270).

Analyzing why customers fail to get hits shows what can be done to improve their success and what is beyond the control of the library. For example an analysis of the types of material sought but not owned has implications for collection development. Customer education or simply better (or more visually appealing) explanations on the screens may lessen confusion about what materials the OPAC contains.

An OPAC screen display for zero hit searches used by the University of Missouri–Kansas City Library (Peters, 1989, p. 268) gives customers suggestions on how to redo their searches to improve the likelihood of a hit. This is an excellent example of a library's interest in educating customers to improve service quality.

BUILDING AN INFORMATION SYSTEM

An old cliché says that organizations never stay the same; they either go forward or backward. As a result, service quality must be regularly monitored to assess whether it is improving or disintegrating. This book differs from others that have attempted to measure library service in that it deals with service elements in terms of their responsiveness to customers and stresses that all employees be involved in assuming responsibility for service quality. Data about response times, equipment maintenance, information services, building maintenance, and customer safety and comfort can easily be tracked over time to assess whether service is improving or not.

Time Series or Trend Lines

The easiest way to keep track of such data is with a computer spreadsheet program. Such programs are readily available and easy to use. It is possible to set up a worksheet to resemble the tables presented in this chapter. For each worksheet, the staff can indicate the initial start date and the information about service pertinent to that worksheet for that time period. Information can be updated as needed simply by adding new data.

The spreadsheet allows the data to be easily cumulated and graphically displayed. The data can also be cumulated and combined with data from other units to present a composite picture of service which the library provides its customers. Table 7.17 is an example of information that has been cumulated over time and combined from various units.

Table 7.17. Service Quality—Quarterly Report

Time period covered_____

Telephone Access

Number of calls to library OPAC _____

Number of busy signals for OPAC _____

% Calls receiving busy signal _____

Number of calls to public service departments_____

Number of busy signals for public service departments_____

% Calls receiving busy signal _____

Downtimes

OPAC Status

Number of days with any downtime _____

Downtime as % of total operating time _____

Number of OPAC terminals_____

Number of days any terminal down _____

Downtime as % of total operating time _____

CD-ROM Status

Number of CD-ROM stations _____

Number of days with any downtime _____

Downtime as % of total operating time _____

Public Printers

Number of public printers _____

Number of days with any downtime _____

Downtime as % of total operating time _____

Photocopiers

Number of photocopiers _____

Number of days with any downtime _____

Downtime as % or total operating time _____

Microform Readers

Number of readers _____

Number of days with any downtime _____

Downtime as % of total operating time _____

Consensus of Observer Groups (Excellent, Satisfactory, Improvement Needed)

Indicate the number of responses for each

Physical surroundings (Photos or videotape)	E	S	I
Noise level is low			
Building is clean			
Restrooms are clean			
Shelves are in order			
Materials are in correct order on the shelves			
Books are shelved, not lying around			
Furniture is not broken or torn			
Places for quiet study are available			

Staff Behavior (Videotape)	E	S	I
Approachable/welcoming			
Appropriate body language and a smile			
Courteous			
Willing to give instructions on using OPACs, etc.			
Responsive to customer request/transaction			
Friendly/pleasant			
Includes user in search process			
Maintains eye contact			
Willing to leave the desk			
Follows through to check if customer is satisfied			

OPAC Search Analysis

	Number	Pct.
By author		
By title		
By subject		
By keyword		
other		
Number of OPAC searches via modem		

Response Times

	Days
Average number of days to reshelve materials	
Average number of days to send an ILL request	
% incoming ILLs for which patron is notified on day of arrival	
Average number of days to place/remove a reserve item	
Average number of days serial volumes are off shelves for binding	
Average number of days to shelve newly arrived serials	

Complaints/Incidents

Number complaints during previous 12 months
Number of incidents involving safety/theft/molestation in previous 12 months

Service Costs

Photocopy page charges
ILL charges (by your library to patron)
Overdue charges per day
Charges for lost/damaged items beyond cost of the material

SUMMING UP

Some may say that data collection activities advocated in this chapter will take too much time or be too costly. Yet, what can be more important to a service organization than to monitor the service that its customers receive? If service quality is not a priority for the library what is—collection building? In these times of shrinking purchasing power and the ability to access information held in a computer thousands of miles from the library, the issue of access versus ownership must address customers, their information needs, information–gathering behavior, preferences, and satisfaction. More than ever, any gap between expectations and services delivered should shrink.

Table 7.18 reviews whose responsibility it is for completion of the other

Table 7.18. Assignment of Responsibility

Table Number	Topic	Who Completes
7.1	Policies	Administrators who oversee policy
7.2	Interactions	Unit staff/Individuals in Observer groups
7.3		Unit manager tallies report for one group
7.4		Unit manager tallies reports from several groups
7.5	Building	Unit staff/Individuals in Observer groups
7.6		Unit manager tallies report for one group
7.7		Unit managers tally reports from several groups
7.8	Shelving	Unit manager records data for a week
7.9		Unit manager tallies data from several weeks
7.10	Telephone	Director's assistant/secretary
7.11	OPAC	System manager
7.12		System staff
7.13	CD-ROM	System staff
7.14	Photocopiers	Circulation/Access staff
7.15	OPAC	System staff
7.16		System staff
7.17	Summary	All Units contribute data to administration

tables depicted in the chapter. It shows that different individuals, from individual units to the director's office, have a responsibility. College libraries, of course, lack the number and diversity of staff and would have to parcel out data collection responsibilities.

Trade-offs between service and cost must be expected, but they can certainly affect quality. Library services are no exception; there are trade-offs. The decision to use students to answer questions in reference-information departments, for example, trades cost for service. Whether the trade-off is a good one needs to be verified by some objective data. Every decision you make about service impacts service quality. Quality influences customers' perceptions of the library, either positively or negatively. Which will your library choose?

Chapter 8

A Critical
Leadership Role

*Do librarians really want to hear what people say and to act on their comments,
given limited library resources?*
                    —Comment of one focus group participant

*Delivering great service, one customer at a time, day after day, month after
month, is difficult.*
                                —Berry, 1995, p. 3

S ervice quality is achieved by librarians throughout the organization
collaborating with one another and being empowered better to serve
the institution's customers. Behind the entire staff are managers whose
leadership encourages, supports, and directs the commitment to quality service and reduces the gap between expectations and services provided. That
leadership must be willing to take chances, to reward innovation, and to
reconsider (and alter as necessary) the roles and responsibilities of the staff.
There is a need to review priorities and redesign work so that the staff are
not forced to do even more with fewer resources. A commitment to improving service quality requires a willingness to: (a) identify, admit, and correct
those inadequacies within the ability and resources of the library to remedy,
and (b) maintain an active dialogue with customers.

Service quality requires continuous data collection and the use of the data
collected—be they quantitative or qualitative—for improving service. With
the attention on quality assessment within higher education, managers
must understand critical issues confronting higher education, address the
evolving role of the library within a changing institution, and link quality

assessment to service quality and the meeting of mission- and vision-related activities. Bergquist (1995) issued an additional challenge:

> Leaders must work effectively with complex issues of authority both inside and outside the organization. They must learn to be comfortable with ambiguity of authority and with rapid changes in the nature and source of the authority they must confront and accommodate. (p. 273)

They must also invest in staff training and development. The literature on service quality consistently echoes the significance of a highly motivated and capable staff committed to improving service. That staff must develop and maintain a high level of institutional loyalty, and work with the managers to ensure that the library operates effectively and efficiently at peak performance (Shaughnessy, 1995).[1]

This chapter briefly discusses the image of the library and four attributes of leadership necessary to support a climate of service quality. The attributes include a willingness to:

- Conduct management-based research studies;
- Take risks (and tolerate risk taking);
- Empower staff;
- Challenge conventional wisdom and the status quo; and
- Redirect organizational resources to offset areas needing improvement.

As also discussed, librarians must replace the focus on inputs and outputs with serious consideration of outcomes and impacts, and quality and questions such as:

- What difference have libraries made to the education of graduating students?
- Do students (and their parents) believe that they are getting a fair return on the investment they are making in higher education?
- Can the library assist in student retention?
- What image does the library project?
- Does that image have a positive or negative impact on the library's ability to accomplish its vision of quality (see Chapter 3)?

Such questions underscore that librarians must address the same issues and concerns affecting many academic institutions.

---

[1] Ironically, in a survey, library staff reported they "perceive themselves to be more loyal to their library directors than their library directors are to them." (Lawson & Dorrell, 1992, p.191)

During the focus group interviews, participants stressed that account-ability of the institution and library was a real matter and not an abstract issue. "In the past," as one librarian commented, "we did not have to be con-cerned about accountability. However, the present fiscal climate, the drive toward privatization of university services, and the demand of the state leg-islature make accountability a real issue."[2] The person further noted that higher education administrators "want hard data on how the library con-tributes to the learning process and student retention." Staff need to be trained, as this librarian and other focus group participants stressed, in ways to gather pertinent data and prepare responses to difficult issues.

LEADERSHIP

The value of a well-trained and highly motivated staff is something that even federal agencies have learned. In a review of quality management in 10 agencies, the General Accounting Office (GAO) found that the agencies were spending more money on employee training and were conducting more in-house training. In-house training apparently reduced costs and enabled the agencies to customize programs and gain more credibility with the employ-ees. Furthermore, increased and direct communication between managers and employees have stimulated the flow of ideas, information sharing, and coordination and cooperation within the agencies. As well, the agencies have developed teamwork approaches to address cross-functional issues, and some agencies have created self-managed teams to carry out certain tasks. Each agency has empowered its employees to be actively involved in improv-ing their work processes, widening their responsibilities, and contributing ideas to improve services. The agency personnel surveyed emphasized the importance of top management support and participation for quality man-agement to be successful (General Accounting Office, 1995).

Turning to the management literature on service quality, Berry (1995, p. 5) offered a "framework for great service" within a company that relies on a service quality information system and a service strategy, and nurturing service leadership. He identified strategies (pp. 7–31) and a checklist of ques-tions essential for cultivating service leadership (pp. 30–31).[3]

The librarians participating in the focus groups recognize the need for a well-trained staff but do not all share the same vision of change and service quality. At one focus group site, we asked, "Does the library have a staff ded-

---

[2] Some universities have already privatized parking, computer center, student union, and health care services. The drive at some institutions to replace tenure with limited-term con-tracts is another attempt to shift costs away from the university's budget base.

[3] Chapters 6 and 7 of this book discuss a service quality information system for libraries.

icated to the same vision of quality and operating at peak performance?" The answer was a resounding "no," but they saw no relationship between service quality and peak performance. A vision that is not "based on understanding the real and meaningful educational outcomes of...(the) institution (Meyer, 1995, p. 335) is detrimental to the library's effective performance.

Service quality must be linked to both the planning process and decision making. Decision making aims to influence value judgments held by other individuals and to change as a planned activity leads to the better accomplishment of the library's mission and higher quality service. It is clear that the profession could learn from case studies of libraries, such as the one at Wright State University, and about how the librarians there developed a total commitment to service quality and how they honor their pledge.

Management-Based Research

As Chapter 2 indicates, librarians could conduct a variety of different types of evaluation studies. Moreover, as Tables 4.2 and 6.1 illustrate, even within the realm of service quality, there are so many facets to consider and explore. Library managers definitely have choices about what priorities to address and must make decisions based on the choices made. A management perspective concentrates on the general utility of study findings to immediate decision making and planning, rather than on understanding the phenomenon at a more basic conceptual level.

As Hernon (1994b) reminded us:

When taking a photograph with a sophisticated camera that requires complex settings, many people might be satisfied with a picture in which the primary target is off-center and perhaps not completely focused. The question is "How much off-center and out of focus is the photographer willing to accept?" Of course, we might all like to have high-powered research data, but realistically we might be willing to accept something less. How much less? (p. 27)

In part, this is a question for library managers and the administrators to whom they report to answer. Chapter 4 dealt with pilot studies with a total of 220 completed survey forms. It is possible that a larger-scale study (see Chapter 5) might have produced different results. Nonetheless, the data collected from smaller-scale studies could provide managers with insights leading to revised policies and practices.

The data collected clearly indicate areas in which improvements might be made (see Chapters 4 and 5). The usefulness of output measures, except for the materials fill rate (examining success in obtaining materials for specific authors, titles, and subjects) is unclear. What can managers do with the data? How can they improve reference service, for instance, by knowing that the staff answer .27 questions per capita (see Goulding, 1991)? On the other hand:

> Suppose that you discovered that 48 percent of your books had the wrong Dewey numbers on the spines, or that 48 percent of the people who come to pick up reserves got the wrong material? As administrators, you would be hitting the roof and willing to spend whatever the cost to identify and correct the problem. How can you go on accepting a 48 percent fail rate in the most expensive operation in your libraries—your reference departments? (p. 109)

Clearly, it is important "to build bridges" (p. 109) between research and management, and management and action.

Focus group participants wanted alternatives to relying on anecdotal data, impressions, and unstructured observation. They wanted to make choices from a list of options and to have easy-to-administer data collection instruments and procedures. They also called for alternatives to the use of surveys and self-reported data. Together, Chapters 4, 5, 6, and 7 offer choices so that staff can pick and choose those that best meet their local circumstances, while demonstrating accountability and leadership.

Risk Taking

As mentioned in a quotation at the beginning of the chapter, one focus group participant questioned whether librarians really want to hear what customers have to say and to take action accordingly. Complicating matters, how often do library managers hire staff who are willing to take risks as opposed to wanting a "safe," comfortable, and secure job?

When presented with Table 3.5, the customer pledge of Wright State University library, two participants in the final focus group were alarmed that a library would make such a commitment. As they asked, "What does the library do if it cannot provide service within the allotted time?" They also wondered how the customers would react if libraries functioned more as a business and charged for their services. Other respondents replied that the library already did charge for certain services.

As the comments indicate, some staff are uncomfortable and unwilling to take risks, but how can those willing to do so be supported? Managers will have to set some boundaries on risk taking but they need to acknowledge and learn from mistakes.

Empowering the Staff

Risk taking calls for a staff empowered to act on behalf of customers and to increase customer loyalty to the library. Empowerment does not mean that managers abandon or shirk their responsibilities; rather, it encourages librarians to be advocates of the library, to solicit information about areas needing improvement, to act on that information, and to feel that they make an important contribution to meeting the mission and vision of the organization. They ensure that library programs, services, and collections "make a significant and positive mission-related difference in the lives of people affiliated with the college or university" (Bergquist, 1995, p. 70), thus making an important contribution to the quality of service provided and, at the same time, gaining self-satisfaction.

Challenging the Notion That "We Always Do It This Way"

Libraries can be rigid organizations in which staff have a mindset on how to do things and assume that they already know what comprises service quality. However, a number of both public and technical service librarians are ready to take risks to better serve customers, while also containing or cutting costs, and capitalizing "on opportunities for innovation" (Ruschoff, 1995, p. 52). They "are responding to austerity with innovation" (p. 56). As the survey findings in Chapter 4 indirectly suggest, customers also value being able to use libraries on their own without having to rely on staff assistance directly.[4] They also like online public access catalogs (OPACs) and the ability to identify what materials have and have not been checked out, and being able to find material in the collection and in its proper location.

By the way, some librarians in the focus groups commented they notice a difference in the type of questions that they receive before and after the introduction of the OPAC. They note that since an OPAC indicates shelf availability, users assume that if an item is not checked out, it will be in the collection in its proper place.

The challenge, as focus group participants reminded each other, is to overcome a mindset that "we always do it this way" or "we have to do it this way because cataloging and classification practices do not permit any variation." As already mentioned, a commitment to service quality attacks the status quo and ensures that the organization changes and thrives. At the libraries visited, the librarians wanted to develop user friendly interfaces for existing electronic services so that users can feel comfortable in

---

[4] Rettig (1991, p. 13) makes some interesting observations about bibliographic instruction (BI). He calls "the BI movement...misdirected" for failing to advance its "rhetoric" and "theoretical discussions...beyond the teaching of a simple strategy to students who may or may not have any immediate or even long-term use for it." Furthermore, BI "is not what people want when they seek library services."

negotiating the system often without outside assistance. Such an attitude should extend throughout the organization and apply broadly to nonelectronic services as well.

Redirecting Organizational Resources

Referring again to the final focus group in which participants commented on general findings from Chapter 4, the librarians reiterated that to engage in change may require additional resources. "Is the library, including all departments, willing to support a reallocation of resources?" Another participant was stronger in her comments: "How many library directors are willing to take risks?"

As the librarians remarked, if customers really want the library open longer, how will library managers get the resources to meet the request? A commitment to service quality would require ascertaining the extent to which customers really believe this and what the library could, in fact, do. In effect, service quality means a commitment to an ongoing dialogue with customers and a realization that librarians must make adjustments to better accommodate customers. Thus, a complaint management system, such as is discussed in Chapter 3, becomes essential.

For us, one of the most surprising findings from the pilot studies (Chapter 4) was customer concern that some libraries are not perceived to be safe places to visit. Such a concern may well require a refocusing of library resources.

IMAGE PROJECTED BY THE LIBRARY

Most often, the librarians participating in the focus groups were either uncertain about the image that the library projects or maintained that the library tries to be everything to everyone. What does it do best, how can it articulate this through its vision statement, and how can it implement programs, services, and practices in a consistent manner? Some participants asked:

- Do we know what business we are in?
- If we do know, how well do we convey this to our customers?

At the final focus group interview, one participant theorized that "At one time we did know the business we were in. Although it was not true, we felt we had control over the literature." As he continued, "Now there is obviously no control. And, it is becoming difficult to find quality among the vast quantity of electronic and other resources?[5] What is our unique role in these times?" Another participant suggested, "In some instances, technology is driving the profession and library schools." As other participants noted, "How does technology affect our image and ability to meet that image realistically?"

Librarians intent on improving service quality, therefore, should review their mission, vision, and image. They need a framework for viewing service quality and setting priorities (deciding which areas needing improvement to address). Likely, the library will have to initiate a (or revise its) marketing strategy to explain what it will and is unable to do.

CONCLUSION

Service quality is a concept the entire organization must embrace if librarians are to resolve problems or areas needing improvement, be truly responsive to the needs and preferences of customers, and "take services to users rather than expecting everyone to come to one place to fulfill their needs" (Hoadley, 1995, p. 175). In effect, both the customers and those serving them must be in sync—reducing or eliminating the gap between expectations and the services provided. Institutions of higher education must also be concerned about quality and access as they must accommodate the changing needs of students who, for instance, are older, working, or parents. As more institutions value student time and compete for tuition monies, access becomes a key issue; for a discussion of the linkage between quality and access see Bergquist (1995).

---

[5] In an interview, Clifford Stoll, a leading computer security expert and advocate of the Internet, voiced his disillusionment with the Internet. He noted:

The information highway is being sold to us as delivering information, but what it's really delivering is data. Numbers, bits, bytes, but damned little information. Unlike data, information has utility, timeliness, accuracy, a pedigree. Information, I can trust. But (for) the data coming across America Online...or whatever, nobody stands behind it. Is the author a medical doctor or some bozo?...What's missing is anyone who will say hey, this is no good. Editors serve as barometers of quality, and most of an editor's time is spent saying no.

Furthermore:

Newspaper publishers are in fear of the Internet. In fear of what? Everybody's losing money by going on line. There's this foolishness among publishers and reporters, just like librarians and school teachers; they are cowed by the technology. They think..."You can deliver immediate information, everywhere, instantly. They're going to cut us out." (Wald, 1995, p. E7)

As librarians embrace a commitment to service quality, and as use of electronic resources raises customer expectations, librarians themselves might complete both surveys, *Service Quality for Library Users* and *Library Customer Survey* (Appendices A and B) and compare the similarities and differences in their perceptions and those of other customers. In the process, they might gain new insights into customer expectations and realign service priorities.

Librarians can learn from "business and industry [and a host of other groups and literatures to]...apply appropriate business [, research, and other] techniques to managing academic libraries. The key is the words *appropriate* and *proper*" (Veanor, 1994, p. 398). As Chapter 3 illustrates, there are different literatures that librarians might examine.

"Every library could improve its services" (Hoadley, 1995, p. 175), and it is time to move from input and output measures to a more customer focus—one addressing areas for improvement. With such insights, librarians can decide how to improve and challenge each unit of the library to reduce or eliminate those problems deemed a priority to resolve. Failure to respond to customers' expectations may have dire consequences in these times of rapid and dramatic change.

Unlike output measures that attempt to provide librarians with an internal diagnosis and a means of external comparison (to other institutions), service quality is intended only to accomplish the former. There is nothing to prevent the adoption of different types of evaluations or process improvements, such as benchmarking. However, can libraries afford not to: (a) focus on their customers or (b) make improvements to better serve them? Some banks are replacing tellers with automated services and are charging customers who do not maintain a certain monthly balance. How do customers react? Do they continue to use these banks or do they take their business elsewhere? Now is the time for academic libraries to follow the example of public libraries, emphasizing service as much as (if not more than) collections. In effect, librarians can rationalize not addressing service quality or doing so half-heartedly, but can they continue to do so as institutions of higher learning are increasingly pressured to change?

Chapter 9

Service Quality:
A Critical Issue
Confronting
Higher Education

Act on the possible while awaiting perfection.
—Bogue & Saunders, 1992, p. 19

Great service is rare, but it is not an impossible dream.
—Berry, 1995, p. 3

T his chapter identifies various issues confronting higher education but considers service quality as one of the most basic ones because it focuses on something we all value but consider elusive—quality. Quality, as defined in Chapter 3, examines both excellence and reducing the gap between expectations and services provided. Clearly, all stakeholders (be they students, parents, industry leaders, state legislators, librarians, administrators, and others) value high quality but want it at a fair price. This book has not assessed price but does encourage others to explore outcome and impact measures that have economic implications.[1]

After highlighting some general issues within higher education, this

---

[1] Although this book has not discussed the economics of information, we do encourage the researchers who build on our initial work to review Tables 4.2 and 6.1 and analyze service quality within a costing framework.

chapter discusses some of the more significant survey findings (from Chapter 4) and offers some concluding remarks about service quality.

GENERAL ISSUES

The fact that the average term of a university president is only five to seven years reflects that there are shifting priorities in higher education and that complex issues and challenges are not easily resolved. Furthermore, it is becoming increasingly difficult to placate different stakeholders and members of the academic community. Affirmative action is no longer taken as a given, and a number of institutions have had to lower their admission standards and discount the value of the education provided—offer more financial aid while lowering expectations for meeting enrollment quotas. In the long-term, such actions have severe, if not dire, implications, especially for private institutions lacking large endowments and dependent on tuition to meet their annual budget.

As more academic institutions seek to broaden the pool of potential students, they are courting working adults, people from disadvantaged minority groups, non-residential students (those who do not live on campus), adults with families, students transferring from community colleges, and more part-time students (see Table 9.1). Such individuals may not want (or be able) to spend much time in libraries due to time constraints and family responsibilities. Furthermore, there is increased need for remedial classes as a number of students are unprepared to undertake a demanding educational experience. There must be an extensive and effective support structure to assist these students in gaining the necessary skills and confidence to complete a degree program, within a specified time period, for instance, five years for the baccalaureate degree.

More universities profess a shift of emphasis from research to undergraduate education. Some of them reward teaching with tenure and advancement, and place teaching on a par with research, publication, and grantsmanship; others do not. Nonetheless, higher education is a business in which universities want a bigger share of the economic windfalls generated by their faculty through patents and so forth.

Another trend is for institutions to consider and adopt new methods for delivering education. They are franchising courses and expanding their involvement with distance education. That education might involve the mailing of videos and computer-based or cable television's Mind Extension University courses. For example, the University of Phoenix offers a master's of business administration entirely via computer and modem to students in many parts of the country. The idea of state universities has broken down, and the delivery of courses knows no geographical boundaries. Libraries serving distance education have special needs and requirements placed on their collections and services. To what extent can these libraries support education occurring off campus?

More institutions are trying to further accommodate customers. They might let prospective students make online applications, send transcripts via the Internet to other schools, make attractive videotapes of the campus to entice prospective students, participate in recruitment fairs, and attract business support of programs and internships.

Institutions of higher education spend more money to support computer services at all levels, including the setting up of laboratories. More courses teach and expect students to be computer literate, and libraries must provide more computer support. Some institutions expect incoming students to have their own microcomputers, and some libraries are even developing

Table 9.1. Profile of Older Undergraduates*

Students 24 years or older now make up a substantial proportion of the undergraduate population, especially in less-than-4-year institutions. In less-than-2-year institutions and in public 2-year institutions, more than one-half of the undergraduates were 24 years or older in 1989–1990. While older students are no longer "nontraditional" in terms of their numbers, as a group they differ from their younger counterparts in important ways that institutions need to take into account as they design their programs and services.

Older and younger students differ in their demographic and socioeconomic characteristics, their enrollment patterns, their reasons for choosing a particular institution in which to enroll, how they combine studying and working, and their use of financial aid. In 1989-90, older students were more likely than younger students to be married and have children or other dependents. About one-quarter of all undergraduate women in their 30s were single parents. Older undergraduates, especially those in their 30s or older, were better off financially than students under 24 years old who were financially independent of their parents.

Compared with younger students, older undergraduates were much more likely to attend part time and less likely to enroll in a formal degree or certificate program. Almost one-half of all older undergraduates worked full time while enrolled.

While older undergraduates as a group differ from younger students in many ways, older students themselves do not form a homogeneous group. They are motivated by a variety of goals, including finding a job, training for a new career, enhancing skills needed for their current job or a promotion, and personal enrichment. They also have different family and work commitments. Consequently, how older students combine work and enrollment, how they choose what and where they study, and how they finance their education reflect these differences.

---

* Source: Department of Education (1995, pp. 47, iii). This report uses data from the 1989–1990 National Postsecondary Student Aid Study (NPSAS:90) and the 1990–1992 Beginning Postsecondary Student Longitudinal Study (BPS:90/92) to describe the participation of older undergraduates—that is, undergraduates 24 years or older—in postsecondary education. It profiles older undergraduates and compares them with younger undergraduates along a number of dimensions; describes the participation of selected subgroups of older undergraduates; and examines persistence and attainment among older students who enrolled in postsecondary education for the first time in 1989–1990.

telecommunications centers in which students and other can use various microcomputer software packages and tap into the Internet and World Wide Web. These libraries, in some cases, are removing or consolidating book stacks to accommodate the development of these centers. Other libraries are installing the electronic connectivity so that students can bring their own computers and make connections to the Internet or use a wide variety of software. Such steps are intended to reduce or at least to control some computer costs for the library.

"The academic library's role in the provision, training, and promotion of electronic resources can be one of leadership and partnership, or passivity" (Channing, 1994, p. 223). PowerUp!, a summer program at Wake Forest University, explored ways to create new institutional opportunities to make incoming freshmen comfortable and knowledgeable about using computers. Such a program enables the library "to highlight its staff's expertise and its...facilities, while strengthening and developing links with faculty, students, and the Computer Center" (p. 224).

Some other trends in higher education include the need to direct sizable sums of money to deferred maintenance, state institutions not receiving as much financial support from state legislatures as in the past, a reassessment of institutional priorities—what programs to offer and departments to retain, a dramatic increase in student–faculty ratios, exploration of ways to provide education more cheaply, and, in some instances, movement away from granting tenure to offering short-term contracts.

Service quality is an issue that touches most of these trends. How can the institution and its library offer excellence and reduce the gap between expectations and the service provided? As is evident, there are just too many opportunities for discontinuity between expectations and services. Unrealistic and unmet expectations may have dire consequences for the institution and library. For example, student retention may present a serious obstacle to the institution, and library collections and resources may go underutilized. The library or particular departments (e.g., government documents) could serve a decreasing proportion of the student body.

Librarians must know the institutional culture, and libraries must be as responsive as other college or university departments. Librarians must also recognize and resolve myths such as those identified in Table 9.2.

KEY FINDINGS

Service quality can be defined by customers, and it has many more components than the literature of library and information science recognizes (see Table 4.2). However, despite responses to the *Library Customer Survey* which indicate that all the statements had some degree of impor-

Table 9.2. Six Myths Concerning Libraries and Their Customers

Clients, especially undergraduate students, cannot articulate their service expectations. If they do, it is to request the purchase of more books and journals.

Some of the focus group participants and audience at the AMIGOS conference made this argument. Both the surveys and pretests with customers reported in Chapter 4 do not support this. They could articulate their expectations. As well, the literature cited in Chapter 3 involving the use of SERVQUAL document similar findings.

Larger collections will automatically result in better service—more satisfied users.

Such an assumption overlooks the underlying processes that have to be fulfilled to make bigger collections available. These processes include timely cataloging (see Page & Reagor, 1994), prompt reshelving, sufficient copies to meet the demand (Buckland, 1975), online public access catalogs specifying availability, and so forth.

Students cannot voice their perceptions coherently.

Those responding to the surveys in Chapter 4 could articulate their perceptions. Among other matters, they noted the unwillingness of some library staff to regard their time as valuable and their concern about safety. At the final focus group interview and the AMIGOS meeting, librarians could readily identify with the safety issue and noted steps that they were taking to cope with a campus-wide problem.

Librarians have an intuitive understanding of user expectations so they need not conduct any research or examine transactional data.

As discussed elsewhere in the book, the literature does not support this belief. The major changes in Table 4.1 that culminated in the development of Table 4.2 related to customer concerns. Once librarians saw the changes, they found them sensible. Service quality attempts to ensure that librarians maintain direct contact with customers and not lose that perspective.

Librarians' views of good service are the same as that of customers.

McDonald and Micikas (1994) showed the major concerns of librarians were: (a) informal guidance in the use of the library, (b) full MARC cataloging, and (c) American Library Association-accredited graduates in most professional positions. On the other hand, customer responses reported in Chapter 4 show that these factors are unimportant.

Customers want to be able to use libraries the same as librarians do.

Librarians tend to believe that users should master library skills. Rettig (1991) and Stoan (1984) disagreed; librarians concentrate on the delivery of source material and have not focused on the delivery of the content of information and data contained in that source material. Rettig (1991, p. 9) considered this as a serious shortcoming.

tance (see Chapter 4 and Appendix B), the components most important to customers are very basic. The audience at the AMIGOS conference related to survey respondents' concern about the library as a safe place. They suggested the perception had validity. Some university libraries, we were informed, have installed video monitors in the circulation area that sweep areas internal and external to the library. Obviously, giving students a feeling of safety is essential if librarians expect use of the facilities to increase or even remain the same.

Another important finding is that accuracy is indeed important. Roberts and Sergesketter (1992) reported a survey of Fortune 1000 executives about service quality had an identical finding: "Speed of response is a close second. Courtesy, easy of access, and one-call resolution were also considered important" (p. 18). Yet, customers are apparently unaware that librarians assume no responsibility for the accuracy of the information presented in the collection and obtained through the Internet (see Hernon & Altman, 1995).

Housekeeping matters (i.e., prompt reshelving, placement of items in their proper location, and keeping equipment in good working condition) are extremely important to customers. Librarians often consider these as low-level or nonprofessional duties.

The associate director of one university library explained to one of us that she really wanted a computer placed at the entrance to the reference area and programmed with a survey so that all customers had to do was stop and enter their responses. Periodically, the librarians would push a button and receive summary results from the customer survey. Although such a wish for "one-stop shopping" is appealing, it is not possible. As explained throughout the book, there is no magic key; rather, librarians have choices. If they decide to pursue service quality, Chapters 4 through 7 identify options. The service quality management system (Chapter 7) is more flexible than output measures, is easier to implement, and indicates actions to take (whereas most output measures do not).

Returning to Table 4.2, the first two sections (information content and the organizational environment) may be more important than staffing characteristics. Customers expressed a desire for self-sufficiency. Rettig (1991), drawing on the literature of library and information science, argued users "approach the library looking for answers to questions, not for lessons in retrieving those documents that might answer their questions" (p. 12). Furthermore, bibliographic instruction programs, he suggested, have emphasized form over content and document retrieval over document use (pp. 9–14). As well, how many of those with a reference question will actually approach reference staff and ask their question?

SERVICE QUALITY

Service quality, unlike output measures, views the library as a system and produces data relevant to each and every department in the organization. Furthermore, service quality is an internal diagnostic tool that is not intended as an external measure. Some of the insights gained might be too sensitive to share with peer institutions. For instance, to what extent do libraries want to share their problems and concerns about student safety?

For decades, library directors, upon retirement, had wanted to be known for the number of titles added to their collection during their tenure. Even today libraries celebrate the addition of the millionth, and so forth, title added. On the other hand, we do not hear about the millionth customer served. Clearly, the ethos of collection over customers has guided libraries since at least World War II. Now, due to trends within academia, such as pressure for greater accountability, there is widespread interest in service quality. Librarians, however, are often not entirely sure what a commitment to service quality entails.

Service quality provides a mechanism to ensure that the library meets the mission and vision of the academic institution. The intention is to meet the information needs and information-gathering behavior of library users without necessarily attempting to change the way users go about gathering information. Clearly, librarians must know the "business they are in," who their customers are, what they need and want, and how they know if they have been successful or failed (Banta & Borden, 1994, p. 95).

Unless librarians do so, the institution may impose its own view of service quality on libraries and define outcomes as the number of (Bottrill & Borden, 1994):

- Courses requiring students to use the library for research projects;
- Items checked out by students;
- Library study spaces occupied by students;
- Library computer searches initiated by students; and
- Students completing their first years without checking out a library book.

Higher education administrators might even query how many times faculty members contacted the library about helping their students prepare assignments, the extent to which library skills are meaningfully tied to the curriculum (Rettig, 1991),[2] and the amount of photocopying performed by stu-

---

[2] Stoan (1984, p. 105) concludes, "Research skills and library skills are neither the same thing nor bear any organic relationship to each other."

dents. The final measure raises the complex issue of intellectual property rights, whereas the other measures define outcomes into terms of extensiveness—number of students using something in relationship to the size of the student body.

On the other hand, administrators might follow the example of their peers at California State University who planned a campus at the old Fort Ord site in Monterey Bay without a library. The presumption was that students and faculty could gain access to "information via computer" without having to use "a traditional library" (Hafner, 1995, p. 62). Such beliefs represent a misunderstanding of remote access to information and the development of the national and global information infrastructures (see Crawford & Gorman, 1995; Stoll, 1995). Access to information requires that information professionals be skilled in navigating the information landscape and making judgments about the accuracy, relevance, authority, and so forth of the information perused.

Service quality does not involve merely accepting whatever the customer has to say or making assumptions about what the customers would say if only they were asked. During the question-and-answer portion following our keynote address at the AMIGOS conference, one university library director argued it was unnecessary to survey customers, after all "We know what they will say: buy more books and subscribe to more periodicals!" As reported in Chapter 4, some customers did make such pronouncements; however, others did not. There is need to combine data collection with a marketing campaign to explain what can and cannot be accomplished, and what progress has been made. The Pittsburgh study (Kent & Galvin, 1977) is a reminder that many titles owned go unused and that use drops off after a few years of ownership. The research of Buckland (1975) and others indicates that few titles account for the majority of use and that libraries can influence circulation patterns by variable loan periods and the purchase of multiple copies of heavily-used items.

Service quality, in conclusion, offers an alternative to the use of output measures. Now is the time to move the discussion and data collection from outputs to internal diagnoses that focus on outcomes and impacts, such as the number of articles published using library resources, the number of books acknowledging the library and its staff, the number of courses using the library and for what purposes, and the impact of the library on student retention, learning, and research. However, attention to both outcomes and impacts, and gaining more support for library services within higher education, requires that libraries consider the importance of housekeeping and reduce the gap between expectations and services.

As Berry (1995) reminded us: "Service quality is integral to delivering value to customers. Value is the benefit customers receive for the burdens they endure. Service quality plays a pivotal role in the value equation by increasing benefits and reducing burdens" (p. 264).

Furthermore:

> Excellent service is hard work, but hard work is not what deadens a job. Dull work deadens a job. So does work without a sense of mission, without the opportunity to learn and grow, and without the opportunity to be and feel successful. Great service organizations build a culture of achievement. And achieving at work is rewarding. (p. 265)

APPENDIX A

**Service Quality for Library Users
A Survey Instrument**

The questionnaire contains ten questions. We would appreciate if you took a few minutes to answer them. The purpose is to provide information about your experiences and beliefs so that we can gain a better understanding of how libraries can improve their service-orientation.

1. While using the university library this year have you encountered any **problems** (*i.e., service failures or areas needing improvement*) with the collections, physical environment, or services?
Yes____ No____ .

2. If you answered "yes" to the preceding question, what was (were) the problem(s)? **(IF YOU ANSWERED "NO" PROCEED TO THE NEXT QUESTION.)**

   A. Collections.

   B. Physical environment.

   C. Services.

3. The library is service-oriented. (Please circle the appropriate response.)

1	2	3	4	5
Strongly Disagree	Disagree	No Opinion	Agree	Strongly Agree

Briefly explain your answer.

4. Please circle your response to the following four statements about service quality:

1	2	3	4	5
Strongly Disagree	Disagree	No Opinion	Agree	Strongly Agree

SERVICE QUALITY MEANS

a. Teaching me to be an independent user.

    1   2   3   4   5

b. Handing me information and/or sources, such as books and articles.

    1   2   3   4   5

c. Both teaching me to be an independent user and handing me information and/or sources.

    1   2   3   4   5

d. The library, always or most often, has whatever I need.

    1   2   3   4   5

5. Other than the points covered in question 4, do you see other attributes to service quality?
Yes___ No___. If you answered "yes," please list them.

6. What do you like the *most* about the library?

7. What do you like the *least* about the library?

8. Name *one* thing the library can do to improve.

9. Are you: a. Student, undergraduate____ b. Student, graduate____
c. Faculty____ d. Staff____ e. Other (please specify):_____.

10. During this school term, approximately how many times have you used the library?

a. None___   d.   A few times per month___
b. Once a day___   e.   Other (Please specify)
c. Once a week___   _____

Thank you.

APPENDIX B

Library Customer Survey

Please share your opinions about how important the following aspects of service are to you as a user of this library. **Circle** the number which indicates the degree of importance on the following scale with *1 being of no importance* and *5 being of highest importance.*

1. The materials you want are in their proper places on the shelves.   1   2   3   4   5

2. The library has the current books and journals you are searching for.   1   2   3   4   5

3. Books and journals are reshelved promptly.   1   2   3   4   5

4. The information you get from library books and periodicals is accurate.   1   2   3   4   5

5. It is clear where help may be found when you are having a problem finding materials or using equipment in the library.   1   2   3   4   5

6. It is easy to find where books, journals, and other types of library materials are located in the building.   1   2   3   4   5

7. Staff help you to use the electronic catalog and indexes.   1   2   3   4   5

8. The library staff are friendly.   1   2   3   4   5

9. You do not have to wait more than a few minutes for service.   1   2   3   4   5

10. Library staff understand the information for which you are looking.   1   2   3   4   5

11. The staff help you find information you need.   1   2   3   4   5

12. The staff answer your questions about library materials accurately.   1   2   3   4   5

13. It is important that staff are available on each
floor of the building to answer questions about
finding materials.   1   2   3   4   5

14. Staff take you where the material is shelved
instead of just pointing or telling you where to go.   1   2   3   4   5

15. Staff mention interlibrary loan as a means to
obtain materials that the library does not have.   1   2   3   4   5

16. Equipment such as terminals, photocopiers, and
printers are in operating condition.   1   2   3   4   5

17. You can print off the information about
call numbers or journal articles appearing on the
computer screens.   1   2   3   4   5

18. The computerized catalog indicates if materials
are checked out or are in library.   1   2   3   4   5

19. Each floor or major area of the library has
terminals in working condition to access the
online catalog.   1   2   3   4   5

20. You can access the online catalog from your home. 1   2   3   4   5

21. You can renew or request materials via the
online catalog.   1   2   3   4   5

22. Study areas are quiet.   1   2   3   4   5

23. The library is open late at night and for long
hours on the weekend.   1   2   3   4   5

24. The restrooms and drinking fountains are clean.   1   2   3   4   5

25. You feel safe in the building.   1   2   3   4   5

Please circle your status:
          undergraduate____ graduate student____ faculty____
          other (please specify):_____

Thank you for your participation.

APPENDIX C

Participants to Phase One (Chapter 4)

The libraries selected for the first phase were chosen for the following reasons: the investigators knew some librarians there; the libraries reflected institutions ranging from baccalaureate-granting to doctoral-granting, and were members and non-members of the Association of Research Libraries (ARL); and were geographically accessible to us. At each of the five libraries included in the first phase, we conducted a focus group interview with 6 to 10 librarians, representing a diversity of managerial and non-managerial positions, and including both public service and technical service staff. In total, 37 participated.

INSTITUTION A

This institution contains a number of branch and departmental libraries, as well as a central facility. Participants came from different libraries, undergraduate to research, and they deal with a wide variety of customers. They do refer to their patrons or users as customers, "realizing that we may provide them with the burger which they request. However, unlike a business, in some instances, we might encourage them to take a salad instead of that burger."

A couple of the librarians emphasized that in the electronic information age, the role of the librarian is changing. Librarians now pull together information from a variety of sources, including the Internet and the World Wide Web. They massage that information and make decisions as to content and format appropriate to the customer. In effect, "We are creating a product." Furthermore, there was a realization that a number of their customer groups pay for use of the libraries of this private institution. "They have expectations," one librarian commented, "which we must try to meet."

In reviewing Table 3.3, the nine librarians offered a number of changes. Because the table tends to focus on customers who visit the library, we asked participants to identify those components most important for a virtual library or electronic information services, for instance, available via remote access. They tended to emphasize the following components:

- Resources—Information content.
  - Accuracy.
- The organization—Service environment and resource delivery.
  - Convenience, including the number of computer ports.
  - Service reputation.

➤ Service delivery—Staff.
>   ➤ Technical expertise—capacity of staff to deal with technical
>   issues and to fix the problem, and how up to date their exper-
>   tise is.

Many participants recognized that the emerging Table 4.1 contains too many variables for them to examine on a regular basis. They appreciated having a comprehensive view of the components to service quality, but supported our efforts to identify the *most important* ones. Nonetheless, there was no clear consensus among those interviewed.

Under "resources—information content," one group of librarians emphasized that, from a customer perspective, relevance, appropriateness of fit, and currentness of content were most important. This group, however, was unsure of the extent to which customers considered accuracy to be important. The second group highlighted appropriateness of fit, relevance, and accuracy, whereas the third group mentioned appropriateness of fit and currentness.

All participants agreed on the components for "service environment—resource delivery" and "service delivery—staff." For the former, they selected "availability/accessibility" and mentioned that location (under convenience) is most important. As they all agreed, "faculty do not want to walk far; they want the information resources in close proximity to their office. They will make trade-offs for the sake of close proximity." For students, on the other hand, location does not have the same importance. "They care more about service." Under "service delivery," they concurred on the importance of determining what the customer *needs* as opposed to *wants*.

In reviewing the two data collection instruments, they offered some modifications and were highly enthusiastic about the attempt to identify areas needing improvement. However, they were concerned that some of the areas might be beyond their ability to resolve. They realized that there might be a need to improve the communication with customers. They viewed the identification of areas needing improvement, at different times, as an effort to produce a type of benchmark data and to reduce the extent to which problems erode service quality.

They regarded the question, "What is the image or images that the customers have of the library or libraries?" as "an excellent one" but did not know the answer. They suspected that the customer's image may not match the one they wanted the library to project. However, they were undecided about what their image should be. They recognized that it might be useful for them to develop a statement of organizational values and build the service image around them.

INSTITUTION B

This institution, located in a major urban setting, has a library which is a member of the Association of Research Libraries (ARL). The six librarians participating in the focus group consisted of managers from both public and technical services.

The librarians offered a few minor adjustments to Table 3.3. For the virtual library or electronic services, they pointed out that service environment does not play a major role, unless customers experience problems in gaining access to the "help" desk or complain about "down" time. For such a library or service, accuracy of information content, ease of use, and currentness become important. For staff at the "help" desk, behavior is important. As well, the library staff must be able to determine what the customer "wants and needs;" "We may have to change some customer expectations, as, for instance, there are limits as to the extent and type of service which we can offer from the World Wide Web." "The information superhighway," as they noted, "is constantly changing and is difficult to monitor. This presents road blocks in trying to help our customers."

In regard to the most important components for "resources—information content," they mentioned accuracy, relevance, appropriateness of fit, and currentness. Regarding "service environment—resource delivery," they stressed "availability/accessibility." Under "service delivery—staff," they mentioned accuracy and speed of delivery (for technical service staff), and accuracy (for public service staff).

They believed it important for the library to develop a vision statement and a statement of organizational values so that they could determine (and respond to) the image or images which the customers have of the library. As they mentioned, a problem is, "We try to be everything to everyone." One participant asked, "What do our customers expect of us," and then he answered the question by stating that "We must train them to accept what we are prepared to give them!" Other participants responded that if such a view became policy, the library might not be used much for research purposes.

They welcomed the attempt to develop data collection instruments to identify areas needing improvement; "Such efforts will enable us to focus on customers and not to have staff intuition and preferences drive our policies, services, and practices."

INSTITUTION C

This doctoral-granting institution and its ARL library are located in the Northeast. The six librarians consisted of public and technical service librarians, managers and non-managers.

They enthusiastically supported our efforts to develop a framework for viewing and measuring service quality, but did not add any modifications to Table 3.3. They concurred with the assessment of the librarians at institution A. The library administration is "more data oriented; it bases more decisions on hard data." The reference librarians assessed how well they understand and respond to the information needs of their customers; "We serve thousands of customers, mainly undergraduates, daily." "Due to the sheer numbers," one librarian explained, "it is impossible to apply a consistent approach to service quality. Furthermore, "We cannot measure service quality for each customer." Nonetheless, he did realize the library could collect either sample data reflective of the population or data that lacks generalizability. In the latter instance, the intention is to gather "sufficient" data to reflect patterns and "enable us to engage in continuous service improvement." After all, service quality, he explained, "focuses on how to treat or serve people; it means that we are people-oriented."

When asked how the reference librarians approached the question negotiation process and decided on the source most useful to that situation, one participant responded, "We give them what they think they want or at least what we think they want." In effect, "We form impressions of people and their information needs and we respond accordingly." Another reference librarian explained, "I know more about finding information than the patron. At times, I want to dazzle him or her with my knowledge." Other participants challenged such a statement as the antithesis of serving customers.

Two members of the reference staff commented that when assisting customers in using CD-ROM and workstations, "The library must have already made a decision about what to include on the screen. However, these decisions should be reviewed periodically." Therefore, as part of making software user-friendly, they want to consider factors such as appropriate screen icons. They stressed that because they are constantly making interpretations, they want insights into service quality to ensure that their interpretations are accurate.

They did not view customers as a monolithic group and appreciated our goal of subdividing this group into faculty, graduate students, undergraduates students, and other differentiations (e.g., diverse ethnic and cultural populations). The goal, as they explained, should be to examine if differences among such groups occur. Furthermore, certain library products and services might appeal to one group more than the others.

INSTITUTION D

The five librarians at this southeastern baccalaureate-granting institution develop and maintain a small collection related primarily to teaching; the library supports the curriculum and somewhat faculty and student research.

In reviewing Table 3.3, the librarians asked that "service environment/resource delivery" be renamed "the organization—its service environment and resource delivery." They also requested that, for clarity, accuracy (within "resources—information content") distinguish between misinformation and disinformation.

They were pleased that the framework (Table 3.3) was flexible and accommodated electronic services and the virtual library. They understood that service quality must continually be rethought as remote access service increases and the library reexamines collections and services. They believed the physical college library building would always exist but that the print collection would shrink and the library would expand its access to networked services and information resources not locally held. As the director, who also took his turn at the reference desk, acknowledged, "We must become information navigators and navigate information within and outside the immediate collection."

Accuracy, they believed, was the critical variable regarding electronic services and information delivery. "It is too easy," they explained, "for misinformation and disinformation to be picked up and unknowingly used." The Internet, as they explained, makes an ever-increasing amount of information available, much of which is not filtered or peer reviewed. The trustworthiness of such information is questionable. Regarding, "the organization" itself, they identified convenience as the critical variable, and, for "service delivery," they highlighted technical expertise or knowledge.

When asked to identify the most important variables affecting the provision and receipt of high quality library service, they chose: appropriateness of the fit, accuracy, and relevance (all for information content); ease of access (for the organization); and ability to determine what the customer needs and knowledge of user needs (for service delivery).

Under the organization grouping, the director would also select "complaint/compliment procedures," especially "redress for receiving poor service."

The director pointed out that at baccalaureate-granting institutions, directors "wear many hats" and have "direct contact with many users." There is no buffer between the director and users, such as at larger institutions having associate directors. Instead, the director is on the front-line and is much more visible to library users than the director of a larger academic library. The director easily gathers impressions but still benefits from having access to "research-based" data; however, such data can be time-consuming or complex to gather.

The director explained that he and his counterparts at other institutions like to examine normative data and compare where they fit in relationship to comparable institutions. They also like to do benchmarking and make comparisons over time. When one of the investigators suggested that service quality might focus on the immediate organization, and limit the amount of external comparisons, the director agreed that benchmarking applicable only to his institution "is perfectly fine."

Although research findings have direct management implications and use, the data collection process must be easy to do, provide benchmarking, and not be costly and time-consuming. The data must "be useful in getting staff to become innovative and change agents." This is especially true, the director explained, for administrators new to the position. Data also validate trends and occurrences. It is important to offer a rationale or demonstrate use patterns and problems to the administration to get more resources. As well, the data should provide feedback to the organization so that it is possible to make the necessary service adjustments or reinforce that "we are doing a good job; we are doing it right!" Data collection also might "feed into the accreditation process." In brief, the director believes evaluation is an important elements for all institutions of higher education, including the libraries.

When asked about the image that the library projects, the participants responded that, since the institution had a clear-cut mission, one focusing on teaching, the library was known for providing access to information, having a staff willing to help get information and interested in what library users are doing, providing access to "good quality" information, and serving or meeting user information needs. Simply stated, the library can provide information, is willing to do so, and is respectful of the user. Furthermore, "The library is not an end unto itself; it exists to provide a service to the institution."

The staff asserted there is a real difference between service quality in a business and in a library. "A business probably wants to understand its customers, the problems encountered and their preferences, and to take corrective action as needed." A library, on the other hand, "tries to change attitudes so that customers will look on us differently." For example, new faculty might expect the library to provide the same type and level of service that they depended on as graduate students working on their dissertations and other research. College libraries have small collections and cannot meet such demands on the collection and staff. Consequently, "There must be an attitude readjustment."

In summary, the librarians reiterated that the evolving Table 4.1 offers a good framework for conceptualizing service quality but it presents too complex a picture for them to apply. For this reason, they liked the idea of focusing on areas needing improvement and selected outcome measures.

INSTITUTION E

The 11 librarians at this focus group represented the main and branch libraries as well as public and technical services. As well, there were managers and non-managers. They reviewed the framework and concurred that the evolving Table 4.1 reflects their understanding of service quality. These librarians believe that they have a primary function to educate students to become self-sufficient library users, be they using print or electronic resources. They realize they also provide information to users but take their responsibility as educators seriously.

Of all the focus groups, this one suggested the most variables relevant to electronic services as having overall importance. They mentioned that, regardless of medium, important variables under "resources" include accuracy, timeliness, degree of comprehensiveness, and packaging. For electronic services, they specifically emphasized accuracy, medium, packaging ("how easy is it to teach someone to use"), and appropriateness of fit. Appropriateness, they believed, encompassed "content;" in other words, use of the World Wide Web, for instance, may lead to a promising source but upon examination that source has no real intellectual content.

For the "organization," they highlighted convenience and equipment, and for "service delivery," they mentioned behavior, communication, and knowledge. However, these components were only relevant when library users made direct contact with staff.

When asked to select, overall, the most important variables, they referred to all variables under "resources," availability/ accessibility ("the organization") and behavior and communication skills (for public service staff) and knowledge of users' needs and technical matters (technical service staff). They also believed it important for all staff to be able to communicate effectively with staff in other units of the library.

When asked about service image, they wanted to be known as "service-oriented." They discussed the idea of a "caring organization" but did not believe such an image matched the management and provision of information. In summary, they liked Tables 3.3 and the evolving Table 4.1, but found the number of components overwhelming. They did appreciate our attempt to identify, as comprehensively as possible, the various components, but regarded it essential for libraries to set priorities.

BIBLIOGRAPHY

Albrecht, Karl. *At America's Service: How Corporations Can Revolutionize the Way They Treat Their Customers*. Homewood, IL: Dow Jones-Irwin, 1988.

Albrecht, Karl & Ron Zemke. *Service America! Doing Business in the New Economy*. Homewood, NJ: Dow Jones-Irwin, 1985.

Aluri, Rao. "Improving Reference Service: The Case for Using a Continuous Quality Improvement Method," *RQ*, 33 (Winter 1993): 220–236.

Arthur, Gwen. "Customer-Service Training in Academic Libraries," *Journal of Academic Librarianship*, 20 (September 1994): 219–222.

Astin, Alexander. *Achieving Educational Excellence*. San Francisco, CA: Jossey-Bass, 1985.

Ayers, Rita S. "Turning Your Vision into Reality," *Bulletin of the American Society for Information Science*, 21 (December/January 1995): 20–22.

Balm, Gerald J. *Benchmarking: A Practitioner's Guide for Becoming and Staying Best of the Best*. Schaumburg, IL: QPMA Press, 1992.

Banta, Trudy W. & Victor M.H. Borden. "Performance Indicators for Accountability and Improvement," in *Using Performance Indicators to Guide Strategic Decision Making,* edited by Victor M.H. Borden & Trudy W. Banta (*New Directions in Institutional Research*, 82 (Summer 1994)). San Francisco, CA: Jossey-Bass, 1994, pp. 95–106.

Barter, Richard. "In Search of Excellence in Libraries: The Management Writings of Tom Peters and Their Implications for Library and Information Services," *Library Management*, 15(8) (1994): 4–15.

Bergquist, William H. *Quality through Access, Access with Quality: The New Imperative for Higher Education*. San Francisco: Jossey-Bass, 1995.

Berinstein, Paula. *Communicating with Library Users: A Self-Study Program*. Washington, D.C.: Special Libraries Association. 1995.

Berry, Leonard L. *On Great Service: A Framework for Action*. New York: Free Press, 1995.

Berry, Leonard L., David R. Bennett, & Carter W. Brown. *Service Quality: A Profit Strategy for Financial Institutions*. Homewood, IL: Dow Jones-Irwin, 1989.

Bicknell, Tracy. "Focusing on Quality Reference Service," *Journal of Academic Librarianship*, 20 (May 1994): 77–81.

Blueprints for Service Quality—The Federal Express Approach. An AMA Management Briefing. Washington, D.C.: American Management Association, 1991.

Bogue, E. Grady & Robert L. Saunders. *The Evidence for Quality*. San Francisco, CA: Jossey-Bass, 1992.

Bottrill, Karen V. & Victor M. H. Borden. "Appendix. Examples from the Literature," in *Using Performance Indicators to Guide Strategic Decision Making*, edited by Victor M. H. Borden & Trudy W. Banta. *(New Directions for Institutional Research*, 82 (Summer 1994)). San Francisco, CA: Jossey-Bass, 1994, pp. 107–119.

Boyce, Bert R., Charles T. Meadow, & Donald H. Kraft. *Measurement in Information Science*. San Diego, CA: Academic Press, 1994.

The British Library. *Code of Service*. London: The British Library Board, 1994.

The British Library. *For Scholarship, Research and Innovation: Strategic Objectives for the Year 2000*. London: The British Library Board, 1993.

Brown, Janet D. "Using Quality Concepts to Improve Reference Services," *College & Research Libraries*, 55 (May 1994): 211–219.

Buckland, Michael K. *Book Availability and the Library User*. Elmsford, NY: Pergamon Press, 1975.

Calvert, Philip J. & Rowena J. Cullen. "Further Dimensions of Public Library Effectiveness II: The Second Stage of the New Zealand Study," *Library & Information Science Research*, 16 (1994): 87–104.

Camp, Robert C. *Benchmarking: The Search for Industry Best Practices That Lead to Superior Performance*. Milwaukee, WI: Quality Press, 1989.

CARL System. *Reports Documentation*. Denver, CARL Corp. October 1994.

Carlzon, Jan. *Moments of Truth*. New York: Harper Business, 1987.

Channing, Rhoda K. "PowerUp! Getting Wired at 'Computer Camp,'" *Journal of Academic Librarianship*, 20 (September 1994): 223–224.

Childers, Thomas A. "Scouting the Perimeters of Unobtrusive Study of Reference," In *Evaluation of Public Services and Public Services Personnel*, edited by Bryce Allen. Champaign, IL: University of Illinois, Graduate School of Library and Information Science, 1991, pp. 27–42.

Childers, Thomas A. & Nancy A. Van House. *What's Good? Describing Your Public Library's Effectiveness*. Chicago: American Library Association, 1993.

Cipolla, Wilma Reed. "The Mission of a University Undergraduate Library: Draft Model Statement," *College & Research Libraries News*, 48 (April 1987): 192–194.

Clack, Mary Elizabeth. "Values, A Process of Discovery: The Harvard College Library's Organizational Values Process," *Library Administration & Management*, 9 (Summer 1995): 146–152.

Craig, Philip R. *A Case of Vineyard Poison*. New York: Scribner, 1995.

Crawford, Walt & Michael Gorman. *Future Libraries: Dreams, Madness & Reality*. Chicago: American Library Association, 1995.

Cronin, J. Joseph, Jr. & Steven A. Taylor. "Measuring Service Quality: A Reexamination and Extension," *Journal of Marketing*, 56(3) (July 1992): 55–68.

Cronin, J. Joseph, Jr. & Steven A. Taylor. "SERVPERF versus SERVQUAL: Reconciling Performance-Based Perceptions Minus Expectations of Service Quality," *Journal of Marketing*, 58 (January 1994): 125–131.

"Customer Service Data: Amasssed But Ill-Used," *Training*, 32 (May 1995): 16.

Dalton, Gwenda M.E. "Quantitative Approach to User Satisfaction in Reference Service Evaluation," *South African Journal of Library and Information Science*, 60 (1992): 89–103.

Davidow, William H. & Bro Uttal. "Service Companies: Focus Or Falter," *Harvard Business Review*, 89 (July-August 1989): 77–85.

Department of Commerce. Office of Consumer Affairs. *Managing Consumer Complaints: Responsive Business Approaches to Consumer Needs*. Washington, D.C.: Government Printing Office, 1992.

Department of Education. National Center for Education Statistics. Office of Educational Research and Improvement. *Profile of Older Undergraduates:*

1989–90. Washington, D.C.: Government Printing Office, April 1995.

Dewdney, Patricia & Catherine S. Ross. "Flying a Light Aircraft: Reference Service Evaluation from a User's Viewpoint," *RQ*, 34 (Winter 1994): 217–230.

DiPrimio, Anthony. *Quality Assurance in Service Organizations*. Radnor, PA: Chilton, 1987.

Disend, Jeffrey E. *How to Provide Excellent Service in Any Organization*. Radnor, PA: Chilton Book Co., 1991.

Donnelly, James H., Jr. *Close to the Customer*. Homewood, IL: Business One Irwin, 1992.

Drott, M. Carl. *Dr. Drott's Random Sampler: Using the Computer as a Tool for Library Management*. Englewood, CO: Libraries Unlimited, 1993.

Durrance, Joan C. "Reference Success: Does the 55 Percent Rule Tell the Whole Story?," *Library Journal*, 114 (April 15, 1989): 31–36.

Dynix. *Management Reports*. Provo, UT: Dynix, n.d.

Edwards, Susan, & Mairéad Browne. "Quality in Information Services: Do Users and Librarians Differ in Their Expectations?," *Library & Information Science Research*, 17 (1995): 163–182.

Elliot, Kevin M. "A Comparison of Alternative Measures of Service Quality," *Journal of Customer Services in Marketing & Management*, 1 (1994): 31–42.

Emery, Charles D. *Buyers and Borrowers: The Application of Consumer Theory to the Study of Library Use*. New York: Haworth Press, 1993.

Forsha, Harry I. *The Pursuit of Quality through Personal Change*. Milwaukee, WI: ASQC Quality Press, 1992.

Freemantle, David. *Incredible Customer Service: The Final Test*. London: McGraw-Hill, 1993.

Galagan, Patricia A. "Training Delivers Results to Federal Express," *Training & Development*, 45 (December 1991): 26–33.

General Accounting Office. *Federal Quality Management: Strategies for Involving Employees*. GAO/GGD-95-79. Washington, D.C., 1995.

Glazier, Jack D. & Ronald R. Powell, ed. *Qualitative Research in Information Management*. Littleton, CO: Libraries Unlimited, 1992.

Glogowski, MaryRuth Phelps. *Academic Libraries and Training*. Greenwich, CT: JAI Press, 1994.

Gorchels, Linda M. "Trends in Marketing Services," *Library Trends*, 43 (Winter 1995): 494–509.

Goulding, Mary. "Minimum Standards as a First Step toward evaluation of Reference Services in a Multitype System," in *Evaluation of Public Services and Public Services Personnel*, edited by Bryce Allen. Urbana, IL: University of Illinois, Graduate School of Library and Information Science, 1991, pp. 103–124.

Grönroos, Christian. "A Service Quality Model and Its Marketing Implications," *European Journal of Marketing*, 18 (1984): 36–44.

Guaspari, John. *I Know It When I See It*. New York: American Management Association, 1985.

Hafner, Katie. "Wiring the Ivory Tower," *Newsweek* (January 30, 1995), pp. 62–63, 66.

Hague, Sir Douglas. *Beyond Universities: A New Republic of Intellect*. London: The

Institute of Economic Affairs, 1991.

Hardesty, Larry, Jamie Hastreiter, & David Henderson. *Mission Statements for College Libraries*. Chicago: American Library Association, College Libraries Section, College Library Information Packet Committee, 1985.

Hébert, Francoise. "Service Quality: An Unobtrusive Investigation of Interlibrary Loan in Large Public Libraries in Canada," *Library & Information Science Research*, 16 (1994): 3–21.

Henderson, Albert. "The Bottleneck in Research Communications," *Publishing Research Quarterly*, 10 (4) (Winter 1994/1995): 5–21.

Hernon, Peter. "Determination of Sample Size and Selection of the Sample: Concepts, General Sources, and Software," *College & Research Libraries*, 55 (March 1994a): 171–179.

Hernon, Peter. *Statistics: A Component of the Research Process*. Norwood, NJ: Ablex, 1994b.

Hernon, Peter & Charles R. McClure. *Evaluation and Library Decision Making*. Norwood, NJ: Ablex, 1990.

Hernon, Peter & Ellen Altman. "Misconduct in Academic Research: Its Implications for the Service Quality Provided by University Libraries," *Journal of Academic Librarianship*, 21 (January 1995): 27–38.

Hinton, Tom & Wini Schaeffer. *Customer-Focused Quality: What to Do on Monday Morning*. Englewood Cliffs, NJ: Prentice-Hall, 1994.

Hirshon, Arnold. "Library Strategic alliances and the Digital Library in the 1990s: The OhioLINK Experience," *Journal of Academic Librarianship,* 21 (September 1995): 383–386.

Hoadley, Irene B. "Customer Service? Not Really,"*College & Research Libraries News*, 56 (March 1995): 175–176.

Humphries, Anne W. & Gretchen V. Naisawald. "Developing a Quality Assurance Program for Online Services," *Bulletin of the Medical Library Association*, 79 (July 1991): 263–270.

International Business Machines Corp. "Annual Meeting Report." Armonk, NY: The author, June 1994.

Johnson, Diane Tobin. "Focus on the Library Customer: Revelation, Revolution, or Redundancy?," *Library Trends*, 43 (Winter 1995): 318–325.

Karp, Raschelle S. *The Academic Library of the 90s: An Annotated Bibliography*. Westport, CT: Greenwood Press, 1994.

Kaske, Neal K. "Materials Availability Model and the Internet," *Journal of Academic Librarianship*, 20 (November 1994): 317–318.

"Keeping the Customer Satisfied," *Library Management*, 15 (5)(1994): 10–11.

Kent, Allen & Thomas J. Galvin. *Library Resource Sharing*. New York: Marcell Dekker, 1977.

Kotler, Philip & Gary Anderson. *Principles of Marketing*. Englewood Cliffs, NJ: Prentice Hall, 1991.

Krueger, Richard A. *Focus Groups*. Newbury Park, CA: Sage, 1988.

Larson, Carole A. & Laura K. Dickson. "Developing Behnavioral Reference Desk Performance Standards," *RQ*, 34 (November 1994): 349–357.

Lawson, V. Lonnie & Larry Dorrell. "Library Directors: Leadership and Staff Loyalty," *Library Administration & Management*, 6 (Fall 1992): 187–191.

Layman, Mary & Sharon Vandercook. "Statewide Reference Improvement: Developing Personnel and Collections," *Wilson Library Bulletin*, 64 (January 1990): 26–31.

Lisoskie, Pete, & Shelly Lisoskie. *Customers for Keeps*. Mukilteo, WA: Business Toolbox, 1993.

LoSardo, Mary M. & Norma M. Rossi. *At the Service Quality Frontier*. Milwaukee, WI: ASQC Quality Press, 1993.

Lucas, Thomas A. "Time Patterns in Remote OPAC Use," *College & Research Libraries*. 54 (September 1993): 439–445.

Lynch, Richard L. & Kelvin F. Cross. *Measure Up! Yardsticks for Continuous Improvement*. Cambridge, MA: Blackwell Publishers, 1991.

Lytle, John F. *What Do Your Customers Really Want?* Chicago: Probus Pub. Co., 1993.

Mackay, Harvey. "Hospitals Could Learn Plenty from Market-Oriented Firms," *The Arizona Republic* (April 9, 1995), p. E6. (Copyright by United Feature Syndicate.)

"Making Complaints Pay," *Library Management*. 15 (5) (1994): 34–35.

Massy, William F. "Measuring Performance: How Colleges and Universities Can Set Meaningful Goals and Be Accountable," in *Measuring Institutional Performance in Higher Education*, edited by William F. Massy & Joel Meyerson. Princeton, NJ: Peterson's Guides, Inc., 1994, pp. 29–54.

McClure, Charles R. "Opinion: So What Are the Impacts of Networking on Academic Institutions," *Internet Research*, 4 (Summer 1994): 2–6.

McClure, Charles R., Amy Owen, Douglas L. Zweizig, Mary Jo Lynch, & Nancy A. Van House. *A Planning and Role Setting for Public Libraries: A Manual of Options and Procedures*. Chicago: American Library Association, 1987.

McClure, Charles R., Douglas L. Zweizig, Nancy A. Van House, & Mary Jo Lynch. "Output Measures: Myths, Realities, and Prospects," *Public Libraries, 25* (Summer 1986): 49–52.

McDonald, Joseph A. & Lynda B. Micikas. *Academic Libraries: The Dimensions of Their Effectiveness*. Westport, CT: Greenwood Press, 1994.

McQuarrie, Edward F. *Customer Visits: Building a Better Market Focus*. Newbury Park, CA: Sage, 1993.

Meyer, Richard. "Focusing Library Vision on Education Outcomes," *College & Research Libraries News*, 56 (May 1995): 335–337.

Millson-Martula, Christopher & Vanaja Menon. "Customer Expectations: Concepts and Reality for Academic Library Services," *College & Research Libraries*, 56 (January 1995): 33–47.

Morgan, David L. *Focus Groups as Qualitative Research*. Newbury Park, CA: Sage, 1988.

Nadler, David A. & Michael L. Tushman. "A Congruence Model for Organizational Assessment," in *Organizational Assessment*, edited by Edward E. Lawler III, David A. Nadler, & Cortlandt Cammann. New York: Wiley, 1980, pp. 261–278.

Naismith, Rachael & Joan Stein. "Library Jargon: Student Comprehension of Technical Language Used by Librarians," *College & Research Libraries* 50 (September 1989): 543–552.

"Not Resting on Its Laurels," *Library Management*, 15 (1994): 38–40.

Orr, R.M. "Measuring the Goodness of Library Services: A General Framework for Considering Quantitative Measures," *Journal of Documentation*, 29 (1973): 315–332.

Osborne, David & Ted Gaebler. *Reinventing Government: How The Entrepreneurial Spirit Is Transforming the Public Sector.* Reading, MA: Addison-Wesley, 1992.

Page, Mary & Melinda Ann Reagor. "Library Processing Practices by Discipline: Are Some Books More Equal Than Others?," *Library Resources & Technical Services*, 38 (April 1994): 161–167.

Parasuraman, A., Valarie A. Zeithaml, & Leonard L. Berry. "SERQUAL: A Multiple Item Scale for Measuring Consumer Perceptions of Service Quality," *Journal of Retailing*, 64 (Spring 1988): 12–40.

Paul, Meg. "Improving Service Provision," *The Australian Library Journal*, 39 (February 1990): 64–69.

Peters, Thomas A. "When Smart People Fail: An Analysis of the Transaction Log of an Oline Public Access Catalog," *Journal of Academic Librarianship, 15* (November 1989): 267–273.

Peters, Tom & R. J. Waterman. *In Search of Excellence: Lessons from America's Best Run Companies.* New York: Warner Books, 1982.

Plum, Terry. "Academic Libraries and the Rituals of Knowledge," *RQ*, 33 (Summer 1994): 496–508.

Powell, Ronald R. *Basic Research Methods for Librarians.* Norwood, NJ: Ablex, 1991.

Powell, Ronald R. "Impact Assessment of University Libraries: A Consideration of Issues and Research Methodologies," *Library & Information Science Research*, 14 (1992): 245–257.

Putting Customers First: Standards for Serving the American People. Report of the National Performance Review. Prepared for President Bill Clinton and Vice President Al Gore. Washington, D.C.: Government Printing Office, 1994.

Rambler, Linda K. "Syllabus Study: Key to a Responsive Academic Library," *Journal of Academic Librarianship*, 8 (July1982): 155–159.

Reeves, Carol A. & David A. Bednar. "Defining Quality: Alternatives and Implications," *Academy of Management Review*, 19 (July 1994): 419–445.

Rettig, James. "Can We Get There from Here?," in *Evaluation of Public Services and Public Services Personnel*, edited by Bryce Allen. Urbana, IL: University of Illinois, Graduate School of Library and Information Science, 1991, pp. 3–26.

Roberts, Harry V. & Bernard E. Sergesketter. *Quality Is Personal: A Foundation for Total Quality Management.* New York: Free Press, 1992.

Rubin, Howard A. "In Search of the Business Value of Information Technology," *Application Development Trends* (November 1994), pp. 23–27.

Ruschoff, Carlen. "Cataloging's Prospects: Responding to Austerity with Innovation," *Journal of Academic Librarianship*, 21 (January 1995): 51–57.

Rush, Sean C. "Productivity Or Quality? In Search of Higher Education's Yellow Brick Road," *NACUBO Business Officer* (April 1992), pp. 36–42.

Rust, Roland T. & Richard L. Oliver. *Service Quality: New Directions in Theory and Practice.* Thousand Oaks, CA: Sage, 1994.

Seymour, Daniel. *Once upon a Campus: Lessons for Improving Quality and Productivity in Higher Education.* Phoenix, AZ: Oryx Press, 1995.

Shapiro, Beth & Kevin Brook Long. "Just Say Yes: Reengineering Library User

Services for the 21st Century," *Journal of Academic Librarianship*, 20 (November 1994): 285–290.

Shaughnessy, Thomas W. "Achieving Peak Performance in Academic Libraries," *Journal of Academic Librarianship*, 21 (May 1995): 155–157.

Shaughnessy, Thomas W. "Benchmarking, Total Quality Management, and Libraries," *Library Administration & Management*, 7 (Fall 1993): 244–249.

Shaughnessy, Thomas W. "The Search for Quality," *Journal of Library Administration*, 8 (Spring 1987): 5–10.

Siggins, Jack & Maureen Sullivan (comp.). *Quality Improvement Programs in ARL Libraries*. SPEC Kit 196. Washington, D.C.: Association of Research Libraries, Office of Management Services, 1993.

"Simmons College Statement of Mission." Boston, MA: Simmons College, January 1994 [unpublished].

"Simmons College Vision Statement." Boston, MA: Simmons College, September 29, 1994 [unpublished].

Sines, Robert G., Jr. & Eric A. Duckworth. "Customer Service in Higher Education," *Journal of Marketing for Higher Education*, 5 (1994): 1–15.

Sirkin, Arlene F. "Customer Service: Another Side of TQM," *Journal of Library Administration*, 18 (1993): 71–84.

Sjolander, Elsa & Richard Sjolander. "A Strategic Analysis of the Delivery of Service in Two Library Reference Departments," *College & Research Libraries*, 56 (January 1995): 60–70.

Spendolini, Michael J. *The Benchmarking Book*. New York: Amacom, 1992.

Stafford, Marla R. "A Normative Model for Improving Services Quality," *Journal of Customer Services in Marketing & Management*, 1 (1994): 13–30.

St Clair, Guy. *Customer Service in the Information Environment*. London, England: Bowker Saur, 1993.

Stoan, Stephen K. "Research and Library Skills: An Analysis and Interpretation," *College & Research Libraries*, 45 (March 1984): 99–109.

Stoll, Clifford. *Silicone Snake Oil: Second Thoughts on the Information Highway*. New York: Doubleday, 1995.

Suchman, Edward A. "Action for What? A Critique of Evaluation Research," in *Evaluating Action Programs*, edited by Carol H. Weiss. Boston, MA: Allyn and Bacon, 1972, pp. 52–84.

Tjosvold, Dean. *Teamwork for Customers*. San Francisco, CA: Jossey-Bass, 1993.

Townsend, Robert. *Up the Organization*. New York: Knopf, 1970.

Twigg, Carol A. "The Changing Definition of Learning," *Educom Review*, 29 (July/August 1994): 23–25.

Van House, Nancy A. & Thomas A. Childers. *The Public Library Effectiveness Study*. Chicago: American Library Association, 1993.

Van House, Nancy A., Beth T. Weil, & Charles R. McClure. *Measuring Academic Library Performance: A Practical Approach*. Chicago: American Library Association, 1990.

Van House, Nancy A., Mary Jo Lynch, Charles R. McClure, Douglas L. Zweizig, & Eleanor Jo Rodger. *Output Measures for Public Libraries*. Chicago: American Library Association, 1987.

Veaner, Allen. "Paradigm Lost, Paradigm Regained? A Persistent Personnel Issue in

Academic Librarianship, II," *College & Research Libraries*, 55 (September 1994): 389–402.

Wald, Matthew L. "A Disillusioned Devotee Says The Internet Is Wearing No Clothes," *New York Times* (April 30, 1995), p. E7.

"Walking in Your Customers' Shoes," *Training*, 32 (February 1995): 16.

Wallace, Patricia M. "How Do Patrons Search the Online Catalog When No One's Looking? Transaction Log Analysis and Implications for Bibliographic Instruction and System Design," *RQ*, 33 (Winter 1993): 239–252.

Walters, Suzanne. *Customer Service: A How-to-do-it Manual for Librarians*. New York: Neal-Schuman, 1994.

Westbrook, W. Michael. "What Are We Doing Here, Anyway?," *RQ*, 33 (Spring 1994); 344–346.

Western, Ken. "Mystery Shopper at Large," *The Arizona Republic* (March 12, 1995), pp. D1–D2.

White, Marilyn Domas & Eileen G. Abels. "Measuring Service Quality in Special Libraries: Lessons from Service Marketing," *Special Libraries*, 86 (Winter 1995): 36–45.

Whitman, John R. *The Beneserve Manual*. Wellesley, MA: Surveytools Corp., 1995.

Wilson, Patrick. "Unused Relevant Information in Research and Development," *Journal of the American Society for Information Science*, 46 (1995): 45–51.

Wright State University Libraries. "Our Commitment to Customer Service." [unpublished]. Dayton, OH, 1995.

Wylde, Margaret A. "How to Read An Open Letter," *American Demographics*, 16 (September 1994): 48–52.

Zeithaml, Valarie A., A. Parasuraman, & Leonard L. Berry. *Delivering Quality Service: Balancing Customer Perceptions and Expectations*. New York: The Free Press, 1990.

Zemke, Ron with Dick Schaaf. *The Service Edge*. New York: Penguin Books, 1989.

Author Index

Subject Index